Disagree
without
Disrespect

How to Respectfully Debate with Those who Think, Believe and Vote Differently from You

Philip Blackett

PREFACE

"To avoid criticism, do nothing, say nothing and be nothing." — **Elbert Hubbard**

"In the practice of tolerance, one's enemy is the best teacher." – **Dalai Lama**

At the heart of any vibrant society lies a symphony of disparate voices, each contributing to the rich tapestry that forms the human experience. *Disagree without Disrespect* delves into the art of respecting our human relationships through thoughtful debate and the celebration of diversity of thought. Within these pages, you will uncover a profound exploration of engagement in healthy disagreement, a beacon of respect amidst the cacophony of voices, even when – especially when – those voices clash.

I was compelled to write this book because I've witnessed the transformative power of weaving unity from discord. Drawing from over a decade of studying business, politics, theology and economics, and infusing the hard knock lessons learned from my entrepreneurial journey and varied life experiences, I have created a map to navigate the troubled waters of polarized discourse. I humbly aim to guide you, the reader, towards mutual understanding and respect, where dialogues conclude not with closed doors and severed relationships, but opened hearts and curious minds.

Imagine yourself at a family gathering where your cousin espouses a political view diametrically opposite to your own, or recall an online discussion that grew heated over a social issue dear to your heart. These moments are not just hypothetical; they are the lived reality of millions of individuals worldwide who, like yourself, yearn for connections and relationships unmarred by discord and disagreement. I have crafted this book with you in mind, knowing the value you place on harmonious relations and the preservation of diversity in thought.

I am deeply indebted to the timeless wisdom of Scripture, cherished mentors, and the historical giants of civil discourse who have inspired the pages that follow. Their insights have granted me the vision to see beyond contention and to understand that every argument holds an opportunity for growth, connection and reconciliation.

As you embark on this journey through *Disagree without Disrespect*, I offer immense gratitude for blessing me with your time and your attention. The dedication you show to expanding your horizons and embracing the beautiful complexity of differing views is a testament to your commitment to building a more understanding, respectful and compassionate world.

This book is intended for those who engage in social, political, or religious discussions with regularity and are seeking to transform conflict into connection. No prerequisites are needed, save for an open heart and a willingness to learn.

Speaking in a manner as if sharing a comforting conversation with a trusted mentor, I invite you to navigate the chapters ahead with the same spirit of curiosity and hope that guided their creation.

Thank you for your investment in yourself and in the relationships of others. Let us journey together beyond the initial chapters, towards the acquisition of skills that will not only serve you in debate but will enrich every facet of your life. It is my sincere belief that the solutions you seek are found within these pages — solutions that foster understanding, patience, and a renewed love for our shared humanity.

CONTENTS

To my mother, Carolyn Wade Blackett, who taught me, among other things in my life, that you can still love someone, even though you do not agree with that person on everything.

***

To my wife, Mayra, and our children who inspire me to help make this world a better place than how I found it, so that we can truly co-exist in a world diverse not only in how we look, but also in how we think, believe, and vote, while still choosing to love and respect one another in spite of our differences.

INTRODUCTION

During the Fourth of July weekend in 2023, some family members joined my family in Boston to celebrate the holidays while catching up with each other. Along with my wife and twin daughters, my mother, sister, brother-in-law, nephew and niece all came together to enjoy each other's company. It was the first time that we had all seen each other in years, as we are all scattered across the United States.

We were having a conversation. I frankly don't remember the topic perfectly. Maybe it was one of those topics that they say should not be brought up at the dinner table: religion, money, politics, or something similar. In any case, when my sister brought it up, I had a strong opinion on the subject matter. Compared to my sister and mother, I am much more conservative within the family. When I started to share my candid thoughts, my mother stepped in and stopped me from going any further. Why? Because she did not want to risk any potential argument within the family get-together that could potentially "ruin" our day because of strong opinions going back and forth.

While my mother may have thought she was doing the right thing by preventing any potential lively debate or sharing of diverse viewpoints that could risk escalating into a full-out verbal fight that could break our family further apart, I honestly felt at odds by myself, silenced from the opportunity for my sister and mother to get to know me even better. Thus, this was a missed opportunity that would prevent us from becoming closer than we are today.

In light of that moment, I realized that what I was experiencing is something that millions of people may be experiencing, and sadly they don't even fully realize it themselves. We live in a world today that would rather silence debate altogether for the sake of "keeping the peace", yet such actions rob us of the opportunity for us to more intimately know one another. It is crystal clear that we all do not share the same views on everything. There is nothing groundbreaking about that. However, many of us choose to isolate ourselves into echo chambers, both in-person and virtually, to repeat the same validating ideas and viewpoints, claimed as "our truth", that make us feel right in our thinking, beliefs and actions. If anyone tries to challenge our thoughts, or simply propose an alternative way of thinking, our society is quick to call that person outside of his / her name, shame the person, or even try to "cancel" that person from any further association with us or with the broader public.

We simply have lost the rules of engagement: the art of debating and subsequently building relationships with those who think, believe, and vote differently than us. Or at the very least, we have become so fragile and sensitive to the point that we cannot even open ourselves up to learn of a different way of thinking. Yet, we call ourselves espousing diversity, equity, and inclusion. However, are we truly including diverse ways of thinking among our family members, co-workers, church members, classmates, friends or acquaintances? Do we provide a sense of equity among each other that your opinion is worth at least listening to and that it has inherent value to the one that possesses such opinion? Are we really about diversity or is it only the diversity that we see externally rather than considering the diversity of thought among those we share community with? Is diversity important only to the degree that it helps further perpetuate our self-interests or the narrative that we want the world to know and adopt regarding us individually or collectively?

I love my mother. She raised me and my sister, with the help of my grandparents and aunt. My mother and me, we do not agree on everything. Clearly. In fact, there are some things that we have decided not to dig deeper on, in order to prevent us from getting into potential shouting matches or not talking to one another on the phone for months at a time. Sometimes, I wish we had enough courage and patience with one another to have the tough conversations with one another in a way that does not push or impose one's viewpoint on another, pressuring the other to accept it or to rebel after feeling threatened. Sometimes, I think we don't have these tough conversations because we do not have the right rules of engagement, so that if we are going to fight, we can at least fight fair.

We live in a world where we do not truly debate ideas on the merits. You and I may have differing views, but why can't we lay out our arguments and take a look from the objective side to see if the other person actually makes sense somewhere in the logic or rationale? You may still retain your overall viewpoint on an issue, but we reached a point where we cannot even give our "opponent" credit without seeming like we have sided – or slept – with the enemy, an "unforgiveable" sin from our peer group, tribe, family, political party or association that we cling to for a sense of identity and acceptance. Instead of merits, we thrive off of appealing to one's emotions and feelings to get people stirred up where they cannot see past their frustrations to soberly and objectively consider the merits of an argument. We would rather interrupt, protest, or obnoxiously silence the opposition from even having the opportunity to speak his or her mind respectfully and openly. And you wonder why we are so divided and polarized today?

We are not seeking some sort of middle ground, even just to hear each other's ideas out without clinging to one side or the other. If there was one thing, though, that my mother taught me that I will always remember is this: just because I do not agree with you, that does not mean that I do not love you. That right there deserves repeating: **just because I do not agree with you, that does not mean that I do not love you**. If we can become a society that does not link love with wholeheartedly agreement, we can become more mature, accepting, and rational adults – and children – that can learn how we can hear each other's viewpoints, debate on merit, wholeheartedly agree in some areas while also respectfully disagree in other areas, and yet still like, love and / or respect one another with the dignity that we all want from each other as human beings bearing the image of God.

That is what this book is about. As much as we complain about how polarizing or divided our world is, let us not forget that we can do something about it to make it better for us and for the next generation. I want to humbly submit to you what I believe is a framework that can allow us to disagree with one another without disrespect. I want to share with you how we can respectfully engage with those who think, believe and vote differently from us. My hope is that this book will help us move the needle closer to where we can have a marketplace of ideas to debate, while still having love and respect for one another, whether we agree or disagree.

1

THE UNITY OF DIVERSE MINDS

On the cobblestone streets of a bustling marketplace in the old city center, where merchants hawked their wares with a fervor matched only by the buzzing of the crowd, Thomas maneuvered through humanity's mosaic. He carried an air of solemn purpose, so starkly juxtaposed to the frivolity around him. Thomas, with a ledger under his arm, was known well in these parts – a businessman with an eye for diverse ventures and a heart for bridging divides fostered by rigid minds.

As he passed a stall of rich tapestries, the scent of dyed wool filled his nostrils, grounding him momentarily in the tangible world. His thoughts, however, wandered, folding and unfolding around gnarlier problems. The market's din receded as he considered last night's board meeting, where voices had collided over the future of the business, revealing a tree of branching opinions. "How, Lord, do we find unity in such discord?" he whispered to himself, a prayer budding under his breath.

Thomas recalled a passage, a kernel of wisdom from the Book of Proverbs, which spoke of plans failing for lack of counsel but succeeding with many advisers. He sought this – a symphony of voices that together could dance towards the light of innovation, rather than churn the dark waters of dissent. A persuasive argument in their shared quest would respect their differences and acknowledge each unique perspective as a note within a greater harmony.

As he strode past a vendor selling freshly baked bread, the aroma tugged at his senses. Pausing, he negotiated for a loaf, exchanging pleasantries – a human connection bridging the gap between buyer and seller. This daily bread, symbolic of sustenance, also represented the myriad grains of thought that together formed a whole – a lesson in life. A child nearby laughed, chasing a hoop with a stick, drawing a smile from Thomas. In such simple joys, were there not lessons of life's beauty in variety?

A nod to a familiar shopkeeper, a brief conversation about the weather, and Thomas continued on, nearing the building where young startup entrepreneurs gathered for weekly mentorship sessions. He would arrive soon, his mind alight with the day's spiritual and sensory stimuli, ready to convey to these budding innovators that diversity of thought was not a chasm to fear, but a patched quilt to weave into their ventures. The young eyes that met him would soon learn the true resilience found in the intersection of differing views and the sustenance of shared purpose – entrepreneurial lessons wrapped in life's greater teachings.

Thomas considered the marketplace, this microcosm of the city's heart, where every exchange was a thread in a larger fabric. Would today's lessons find fertile soil in the minds of the young and impressionable? Could they, in time, cultivate a business landscape rich with diversity - not just in how people looked like on the outside but also how people thought and believed on the inside, bearing the fruit of a collective wisdom? How many lives would be touched by the hands that learned to build bridges over the rivers of dissent and disagreements?

Together We Thrive

At the core of civil discourse lies the fundamental need for a mosaic of ideas, a crucible within which varied perspectives collide and coalesce, forging pathways for innovation and communal insight. Embracing diversity of thought is not merely polite rhetoric aimed at smoothing the edges of conversation; it is an indispensable engine for societal development. As we forge ahead into this exploration, let us acknowledge that encountering different viewpoints can often be abrasive and uncomfortable, yet it is this very friction that polishes our understanding and broadens our intellectual perspective.

The pages ahead are dedicated to unwrapping the notion that each diverse perspective holds a pivotal role in creating a more harmonious society. **In the ambiance of today's polarized environment, the act of actively listening and genuinely considering an opposing idea becomes a revolutionary one.** Understanding the critical role of embracing diversity of thought forms the cornerstone of any civil discourse. It is akin to the way multiple instruments, each with their distinct timbre and tone, come together to form a symphony. **The very essence of democracy and progress relies on our ability to debate, deliberate, and diverge in thought, without fragmenting the bonds of our shared humanity.**

It is within the crucible of conflicting ideas that society finds its stride for growth and transformation. Diversity of thought propels us forward, challenging the status quo and prompting innovation. Societal growth and personal enrichment stem from our collective ability to value and harness the breadth of human perspective. As the Bible counsels in Proverbs 27:17, *"As iron sharpens iron, so one person sharpens another."* Our collective wisdom is honed through the rigorous examination and mutual exchange of our varied insights and opinions.

Yet, this book is more than a call to understand — it's an invocation to action, inciting readers like you to engage actively in conversations that may test each other's convictions while maintaining civility and respect. **Transforming potential conflicts into opportunities requires a tactful approach, sincere empathy, and a commitment to cultivating common ground**. Herein lies not just the capacity but the imperative to turn discord into dialogue, connecting us across the chasms of our disagreements.

The pathway to mastering the art of debate, especially amidst strongly divergent viewpoints, is akin to navigating a complex tapestry of human emotion and logic. Readers will be introduced to my five-step framework for respectfully disagreeing with others, a methodology that transcends the superficial and dives deep into the substance of constructive conversation. This book is a die cast in the endeavor to maintain personal relationships, promote a culture of tolerant discourse, and shape the landscape of conversation in a way that echoes the loftiest of spiritual and intellectual ideals.

Moreover, with an understanding of these principles, the entrepreneurial spirit finds fertile ground. In business as in broader society, the clashing of distinct ideas, when handled with finesse, can be the lifeblood of innovation and leadership. This narrative weaves the spiritual principles with tangible strategies — a lighthouse for navigating the oft-turbulent waters of contentious discourse. **Let this be a helpful resource for those who seek not only to defend their own positions but to understand the contours of opposing landscapes with grace and nuance.**

In these pages, readers are not passive recipients but engaged participants, learning essential skills for life's myriad arenas. Whether one engages in the boardroom, the town hall, on social media or in the dining room, the principles within are crafted for application across the spectrum, to elevate the collective conversation and to facilitate a growing renaissance of understanding in a world thirsty for ways to navigate a polarized environment where people rather cancel you than listen to you if you do not agree with them on everything.

The fabric of civil discourse is woven from a multitude of threads, each representing a diverse viewpoint and background. In this intricately connected world, the strength of our collective conversation hinges on our ability to embrace this diversity of thought. Engagement in civil discourse isn't merely a pleasanter alternative to abrasive conflict; it is the lifeblood of a thriving community and a resilient society.

Amidst today's polarized landscape, it's essential to recognize that each individual's perspective is a vital component of the larger dialogue. These differing viewpoints are not anomalies to be corrected but treasures to be valued. Much like a masterfully composed symphony, our social harmony demands the inclusion of various notes and rhythms – often counterpointing yet always enriching when played in concert. It is here that we find profound resonance, not in the echoes of a single note but within the chorus of varied voices.

To uphold this ideal in our interactions, we must cultivate a practice of patient listening and respectful acknowledgment. It is a commitment that requires discipline, as the instinct to dismiss or undermine those who challenge our viewpoints can be a powerful and tempting deterrent. Yet, embracing these diverse perspectives is akin to opening doors to a broader spectrum of potential solutions and insights. It enlivens our understanding and can dramatically transform the nature of our conversations – from battlegrounds to collaborative workshops where the best ideas are forged in the crucible of collective wisdom.

The Bible reminds us: *"Blessed are those who find wisdom, those who gain understanding, for she is more profitable than silver and yields better returns than gold"* **(Proverbs 3:13-14), and what better way to accumulate such wealth than through the counsel and consideration of others?** The Book of Proverbs demonstrates the value of a multitude of counselors, suggesting that decisions reached through collaborative deliberation are stronger and more enduring. This is as true for the boardroom as it is for the community center – gathering a diversity of perspectives is a principle that underpins both moral and strategic success.

So why is it that engaging with opposing viewpoints is increasingly perceived as an ordeal rather than as an opportunity? **Perhaps we have lost sight of the fundamental truth that our individual growth is intricately linked to our interactions with others. By drawing others into our decision-making process and considering their opinions, we not only temper our convictions but also cultivate a more holistic understanding of the issues at hand and how best to solve them.** This process is emblematic of a spiritually mature approach, one that values discernment and communal upliftment over ego-driven isolation and winner-takes-all mentality.

In business, as in life, the leaders who stand the test of time are those who harness the dynamism of diverse thinking. They are the ones who actively seek out advisers who will challenge their present assumptions and suggest alternatives. This practice is far from a sign of weakness; it denotes a remarkable strength of character and a resolute commitment to excellence. Moreover, an environment that celebrates diverse perspectives inevitably fosters innovation and adaptability – qualities indispensable in an ever-evolving market globally.

Navigating the Vibrant Tapestry of Human Thought

By integrating an expansive range of insights, from theological to the political and to the economic, we create a rich tapestry of human thought that not only encourages us but also compels us to evolve. The challenge before us is to weave these strands into a cohesive whole without diminishing their unique colors and textures. Through dedicated practice and an open heart, we can learn to savor the vibrancy that comes from truly listening and engaging with the spectrum of ideas that animate our world. It is within this context that we find our next steps, not just as individuals seeking personal growth, but as a society striving towards unity and progress.

The Necessity of Multiple Opinions

A garden flourishes with a variety of plants, each contributing unique beauty and function to the whole ecosystem. Similarly, our society thrives when it embraces a rich tapestry of opinions and perspectives, as opposed to silencing, demeaning or canceling those who think differently. The Scriptures teach us that wisdom comes from a multitude of counselors. In a business context, this principle is paramount; companies that seek out and incorporate diverse viewpoints are more innovative and resilient. Think of the roundtable discussions where varying ideas stimulate breakthrough solutions. Such is the dynamic created by the multiplicity of opinions—necessary not just for organizational success but for individual and team fulfillment.

Personal wisdom grows through interaction with differing viewpoints. Encountering diverse perspectives challenges our preconceptions and prejudices, while it also broadens our understanding. Reflecting on teachings across spiritual traditions, we find a common thread: the value of learning from others. This is a truth that applies with equal force in our professional lives. As we respect and consider alternative views presented by colleagues and clients, we develop a more nuanced approach to problem solving, negotiation, and innovation.

Bridging the Gap Between Perspectives

In political arenas, listening to the other side is often portrayed as a sign of weakness or even betrayal, but I assert this is a misinterpretation of strength. **True fortitude lies in the capacity to engage with opposing views thoughtfully and respectfully**; it is through this process that societies find balance and progress. Economist Adam Smith's vision of a market free and full of varying opinions is akin to a thriving democracy enriched by diversity. Every notion, from the radical to the traditional, holds the potential to contribute valuable insights to envelope into a potential solution that can lead to greater results than either idea on its own. However, we cut ourselves from that possibility simply by not listening intently to the other side. This doesn't merely apply to national policy; within the walls of a corporation, a marketing strategy or product development can be vastly improved by incorporating a range of perspectives and expertise from different people, as well as different departments (i.e. customer service or sales).

The Contribution to Conflict Resolution

Conflict is habitual and inevitable in any setting where opinions differ, but it does not have to be destructive or toxic. Engaging with an array of thoughts encourages empathy and fosters resolutions that accommodate a wider spectrum of needs and desires. When Jesus mentions how blessed are the peacemakers in his Sermon on the Mount (Matthew 5:9), he points out how those who graciously navigate conflict to find harmonious outcomes serve as examples to us of the power of mediation. In business negotiations, the same principle holds. When we approach conflicts as opportunities to understand and to integrate different viewpoints, we often find innovative solutions that were previously obscured by a singular perspective.

Enrichment Through Diversity

In personal development, the importance of encountering a variety of ideas cannot be overstated. Each new viewpoint can offer a stretch of our intellectual boundaries and an expansion of empathy. The enrichment that comes from this exposure is an essential component of becoming a well-rounded human and professional. In essence, it equips us to become better listeners and communicators, roles that are critical in every path of life, from business to the spiritual.

Fostering Innovation and Creativity

Take any historical innovation — the chances are that it was the product of unconventional thinking, a divergence from the status quo. Diverse opinions are the bedrock of creativity and innovation. The encouragement of different perspectives lays the groundwork for the sort of creative friction that sparks innovation. **The cross-pollination of ideas across different fields can lead to the kind of disruptive developments that redefine industries and businesses.** In this sharing and meshing of perspectives, new concepts emerge, leading to breakthrough products or services that benefit society at large. Think about it. If it was not for different viewpoints from the status quo, we likely would not enjoy the benefits of traveling by automobile, lighting our houses with electricity, or exploring the Internet and talking to people around the world by smartphone.

Strengthening Society's Foundations

Our society's foundation is strengthened not by uniformity but by the acknowledgment and integration of different opinions. As we navigate the complexities of the modern world, the collective intelligence gleaned from multiple perspectives is indispensable. It empowers us to build more resilient families, communities, businesses, economies, organizations and institutions. The integration of a variety of expertise and experiences results in better decision-making and more robust policies and strategies, which are crucial for the sustainable development of any society.

Preparing for the Future

The future holds unknown challenges that will require unheard-of solutions. **To equip ourselves for what lies ahead, we must foster an environment where diversity of thought is not only accepted but actively sought.** This approach enriches our lives, fuels continual learning, and ensures that we can weather the storms of change together. By valuing and incorporating the spectrum of opinions that surround us, we prepare not only for the challenges of today but lay the groundwork for a future that is vibrant, adaptable, and more inclusive.

When confronting divergent perspectives, it's imperative to approach discussions with an openness to learn. **This openness doesn't imply wavering on your convictions but rather signals the maturity to recognize that each person's experience colors their viewpoint in unique ways.** In settings ranging from the classroom to the family dinner table, embracing this principle facilitates not only a calmer exchange of ideas but often leads to innovative solutions. Recognizing shared humanity, spiritual teachings emphasize the value of every individual's insight, no matter how disparate from our own. We are reminded that our interactions, including those laced with disagreement, are opportunities for mutual growth and refining of our character as well as our intelligence.

Transforming potential conflicts into avenues for connection begins by acknowledging that all perspectives can coexist within the broader tapestry of discourse. **The ability to listen, truly listen, even when predisposed to resist, is an admirable quality that businesses, organizations, and leaders worldwide recognize as a hallmark of great minds. When individuals feel heard and understood, they're more inclined to engage constructively with you.** John 13:34 underscores this approach: *"A new command I give you: Love one another. As I have loved you, so you must love one another."* In this light, conversations become less about winning and more about understanding and cooperating with love and respect for the other person, even if you disagree with each other.

Engaging respectfully with opposing viewpoints often leads to discovering common ground, where collaboration emerges as a natural byproduct. **The contextual frame is no longer "*us* versus *them*" but rather "*we* pursuing a shared objective." Indeed, resolving conflicts is more productive when we consider our "opponents" as potential allies rather than adversaries.** This shift in perspective can reveal paths to compromise that satisfy more than our individual desires, aligning with the wisdom of Ecclesiastes 4:9, *"Two are better than one, because they have a good return for their labor."* Recognizing the unique strengths each person brings to the table and combining them can create results that far surpass what we could achieve alone.

It's also vital to embrace humility and the acknowledgement that our own knowledge is not absolute. We are just as human as the other person. We are not God. We do not know everything. The moment we concede that we don't know everything is the moment we become open to new learning and perspectives. **The humility and maturity to reconsider our position, informed by facts, new information and other viewpoints, is not a weakness but a strength that is becoming more and more unique today.** In business and personal development, this quality is often the difference between stagnation and growth. From a spiritual standpoint, the reminder from James 4:6 that *"God opposes the proud but shows favor to the humble,"* reflects the importance of humility in all our interactions.

To truly transform conflicts into connections, it's essential to develop the skill of managing our emotional reactions. In the heat of a debate, maintaining composure is often challenging. However, **the discipline to respond, rather than react, adds authority and credibility to any discussion or debate. It allows for a deliberate and thoughtful exchange, facilitating an environment where all participants feel safe to express their candid thoughts.** In this calm space, as 2 Timothy 1:7 tells us, we are not given a spirit of fear, but of power, love, and self-control. Exercising control over our reactions creates an atmosphere conducive to mutual respect and understanding.

In the quest to turn disagreements into dialogues, ask probing questions to deepen insight into the other party's logic.

Questioning not only clarifies intentions and uncovers the reasoning behind assertions but also demonstrates a genuine interest in understanding the other viewpoint. It's a testament to the Socratic method, which encourages critical thinking through questioning, and it is deeply respectful of the intelligence and worth of every participant in a conversation. **Questions can disarm conflict, build rapport, and most importantly, pave the way to a resolution grounded in a holistic understanding of the matter at hand.**

Finally, remember that every conversation has the power to create a lasting impact. **A constructive dialogue, handled with grace and wisdom, can strengthen relationships, inspire trust, and foster a culture where varying opinions are not just accepted but valued.** Such cultural shifts ripple out to affect not only individual relationships but also organizational dynamics and societal norms. **With every respectful exchange, we inch closer to a world where diversity of thought is not just tolerated but celebrated as vital to collective progress.** As we embark on these interactions, let the advice of Colossians 4:6 resonate with us: *"Let your conversation be always full of grace, seasoned with salt, so that you may know how to answer everyone."* In fostering an atmosphere where **every voice matters**, we can indeed transform our various, often clashing melodies into a harmonious symphony of progress and innovation.

The Imperative of Varied Perspectives in Constructive Dialogue

Understanding the criticality of embracing diversity of thought in civil discourse is akin to recognizing the need for various parts of the body to function harmoniously. Each opinion, like a part of the body, serves a purpose, contributing to the whole's health and vitality. Such understanding echoes the spiritual principle that we are many parts but one body and must respect and value each distinct member for their unique contribution.

In the chapters ahead, we will delve into how a multiplicity of opinions acts as the bedrock for societal advancement and personal growth. As iron sharpens iron, so one person sharpens another; the engagement with varied perspectives hones our intellect and compassion. The wisdom of this ancient proverb underscores the forthcoming journey, promising to enrich your understanding and ability to navigate complex social terrains.

Transforming Conflict into Connection

The art of transmuting potential conflicts into opportunities for connection and mutual understanding is not only a skill but a calling to higher purpose. Biblical teachings remind us that where there is unity, God commands a blessing. Thus, we learn to approach discord not with trepidation but with the expectation of finding common ground and achieving progress, as well as blessings.

Unlocking the Potential Ahead

Looking forward to the lessons and insights that await you, consider the heightened clarity and effectiveness with which you will approach debates in your professional life after reading this book. Imagine having the tools to transform heated arguments into constructive, solutions-oriented discussions. The satisfaction of leading by example, using respectful debate to inspire change and spur innovation, will be one of the many rewards garnered as you traverse these pages.

Your Journey Begins

Embark on this adventure with both eager anticipation and solemn reflection. You are not merely adding to your intellectual arsenal but embodying the very essence of what it means to thrive in a diverse world with the proper toolkit and skillset to change the way you forever interact with those who agree with you, as well as those who disagree with you. Each chapter will serve as a stepping stone towards a more enlightened approach to engagement with others, an approach that values differences as opportunities for learning and growth.

Answering the Call to Leadership

The teachings in this text are not merely academic exercises but include guidance and action steps that you can start implementing as soon as you finish reading them in your next conversation, disagreement or debate. As you move forward, you will discover how to imbue even the most heated debates with a spirit of cooperation and mutual respect. This book will serve as your humble resource guide, transforming your discussions and decisions into catalysts for positive change.

In embracing this journey, you demonstrate leadership and commitment to **a world that desperately needs voices like yours — voices that can dissent harmoniously and advocate passionately while maintaining the delicate balance of a respectful discourse**. Step boldly into this exploration, confident that the skills and knowledge you acquire will serve you, your community, and indeed, the very fabric of our global society.

The *Disagree without Disrespect* Five-Step Framework: How to Respectfully Debate with Those who Think, Believe and Vote Differently than You

1. Separate the idea (or belief) from the person who supports it

2. Disagree with the idea (or belief); love the believer

3. Focus on debating the merits of the idea in question (no name-calling, overdramatic emotional reactions) while actively listening to the opposing viewpoint to understand it better

4. Be a good sport whether you change sides, your debate partner changes sides, or neither changes sides or a new alternative is produced after the conclusion of the discussion or debate

5. Affirm your respect, love and / or appreciation for the other person afterwards, regardless of the outcome of the debate, respectfully disagreeing while respecting the diversity of thought

2

RESPECT BEYOND AGREEMENT

On a brisk autumn morning in the quaint outskirts of Richmond, Virginia, Alicia, seasoned in the art of conversation, found herself preparing for an exchange that would test her convictions and her patience. In the fabric of the gentle breeze that whispered through ochre leaves, she contemplated the approaching town hall meeting. High stakes, differing opinions on policy change — a setting primed for discord.

Inside the café that had become her solace before such events, the scent of freshly baked bread and the murmur of friendly chatter anchored her in the moment. Alicia's hands moved methodically, organizing her notes, a mosaic of data, anecdotes, and strategic reminders to remain composed. The sound of turning pages provided a rhythm to her preparation, each flip a step closer to the arena of ideas.

Across from her, an elderly gentleman sipped his tea, eyes closed, perhaps in meditation or prayer. It brought to mind the teachings of her youth, where she learned that respect was akin to a sacred offering — a gift not contingent upon agreement but a testament to the humanity shared between souls. It was a principle she intended to embody fully today, despite the anticipated tension. "Peace be still," she thought, recalling a scripture that felt both like armor and an anchor.

Alicia's entrepreneurial spirit stirred within her, the same spirit that held her steady when she first pitched the community garden project, a venture now thriving and emblematic of her commitment to growth, both literal and figurative. She had learned then, as she recognized now, the power of motivation — to galvanize support, to bridge divisions, and to plant seeds in the fertile soil of open minds.

She left the café, her footsteps echoing with purpose along the cobblestone path. The leaves rustled, as if sharing whispered wisdom of past seasons, of times when respect was the currency of exchange, more valuable than any coin — a lesson apparent in nature's splendid diversity. This morning, she sought to be the custodian of that legacy.

As Alicia entered the town hall, the hum of voices grew — a mixture of concern and aspiration, each thread a voice waiting to be heard. Her resolve solidified. She knew her role today was not just to convince, but to listen, to find the strength in others' words, to respect the convictions behind them, and to weave a dialogue that fortified the community's foundation.

But as she prepared to step into the fray, a thought lingered, an inquiry that echoed in the minds of many who have ever sought to bridge divides: How can we maintain the strength of our convictions while allowing the grace of respect to illuminate our shared journey?

From Confrontation to Agreement: Redefining Relationships Amid Disagreement

In a world rife with such extreme polarization, the capacity to differentiate between respect and agreement has become a cornerstone of constructive discourse. Delving into the myriad of perspectives, this approach is not just advisable but essential in fostering a culture where diversity of thought isn't merely tolerated but celebrated. Respect anchors in the understanding that every person's voice is inherently valuable, regardless of its agreement with our own beliefs. In spaces where ideas battle for supremacy, maintaining civility is not just a moral imperative, it's a strategic one. It facilitates the kind of dialogue that can transform the seething tides of opinion into a mosaic of collective wisdom.

This chapter sets the foundation for recognizing that **agreement is not a prerequisite for respect in any encounter, professional or personal**. Within these pages, patterns emerge, parallels are drawn from the teachings of respected spiritual texts, where kindness and patience exemplify strength, not acquiescence. Let it be a reminder, drawing from Proverbs 15:1, that *"A gentle answer turns away wrath, but a harsh word stirs up anger."* Even in the throes of disagreement, this wisdom echoes the necessity of temperance and respect.

You will find strategies to preserve civility and respect, even as the landscape of discussion grows more treacherous. A prime example lies in the ever-demanding world of entrepreneurship, where leadership necessitates an unwavering respect for diversity. In the cutthroat cacophony of the free market, one must learn to focus not on winning every debate, but on winning trust and understanding through graceful perseverance.

An entrepreneur's journey is often paved with contention, yet it is through decoupling personal value from shared perspectives that one may engage in valuable exchanges without the heat of personal affront. Let us take guidance from the Bible that implores us to *"be quick to listen, slow to speak and slow to become angry"* (James 1:19). The mastery of this artful balance is a testament to a person's ability to engage with wisdom and decorum.

The narrative herein moves beyond mere instruction and into the realm of application, exploring real-world experiences and practical exercises designed to equip individuals with the finesse required to converse with **grace under fire**.

By viewing disagreement through a lens of mutual respect, it becomes possible to unearth common ground and, in doing so, create bridges where walls once stood. Be inspired to action, encouraged to persist in the face of adversity, and emboldened to stand firm in your convictions while embracing the varied convictions of others. This is not just about maintaining composure in the battleground of ideas; it's about shaping a world where thoughtful debate is the conduit for innovation and progress.

In the arena of ideas and discussions, a significant realization must dawn upon us — the notion that respect is inextricably tied to agreement is a mistaken one. **History and faith traditions alike echo the timeless principle that while opinions may clash, the fundamental respect for the person voicing an opposition can, and should, remain undiminished**. Texts from various faiths underline this sentiment, oftentimes urging followers to **treat others with kindness and dignity, irrespective of contrasting views.**

Respect is an expression of our highest virtues — **a commitment to see another person as a worthy individual made in the image of God, capable of intelligent thoughts worth considering, deserving of courtesy, dignity and respect.** In the business world, respect forms the cornerstone of successful partnerships and negotiations; it fosters a climate where ideas can be exchanged freely, and innovation flows from constructive discourse. **True respect lays down the sword of our own biases and picks up the shield of impartial consideration, guarding not only the self but the sanctity of the open exchange.**

However, achieving such a disposition does not come easily, especially when dialogue turns to areas of personal conviction or pressing social issues that can make us feel emotionally charged. We must consciously cultivate respect amidst disagreement. This cultivation is akin to developing a muscle through exercise — it strengthens over time with consistent use and challenges. Consider the entrepreneur who, in the face of skepticism from colleagues or stakeholders, chooses to **listen actively and respond thoughtfully, rather than react defensively**. Such behavior not only reinforces personal growth but also sets an example of composure and integrity.

To navigate these treacherous waters of conflict, look to the wisdom of experienced leaders and thinkers. They attest to **the strength found in maintaining poise and composure when challenged**. Their anecdotes reveal that the most fruitful conversations often stem from contexts where **mutual respect prevails over total agreement**. It is this environment that encourages the sharing of perspectives, ultimately leading to well-rounded decision-making and innovation.

Maintaining civility and respect despite dramatic differences in opinion is a strategic skill akin to a navigational compass in the vast ocean of discourse. It points towards productive dialogue and keeps us from veering into the tumultuous waters of animosity. Remember that each person's viewpoint is a culmination of unique life experiences, knowledge, emotional feelings and logical reasoning. Therefore, recognizing the intrinsic value of diverse thought processes reflects wisdom and maturity, both in personal interactions and in broader social engagements.

Being articulate about boundaries is vital when fostering respectful communication. **Set the tone for discussions by establishing a clear expectation for mutual respect, and be prepared to gently remind counterparts of this agreement should conver-**

sations take a heated turn. It's not about muting passionate advocacy or robust debate; rather, it's about ensuring the undercurrent of respect is never absent from the dialogue.

In practice, **this approach facilitates a climate where individuals feel heard and valued, irrespective of the divergence in views**. Real-life scenarios underscore the effectiveness of this principle. For instance, in high-stakes negotiations or professional team meetings, addressing opposing viewpoints with acknowledgment and without disparagement can fuel more nuanced, creative and inventive solutions. Approach disagreement not as a battle to be won, but as an **opportunity for broader enlightenment and mutual understanding**.

Elevating Discourse: Strategies for Staying Respectful When Opinions Collide

Maintaining Civility in the Face of Disagreement

As we seek to foster an environment where diversity of thought is not only tolerated but celebrated, one truth becomes clear: **civility is the bedrock upon which productive dialogue is built**. This doesn't imply that every discussion is devoid of passion or intensity — indeed, deeply held beliefs often evoke strong emotional responses. However, **ensuring that these exchanges remain respectful hinges on our ability to prioritize the relationship over the rivalry of ideas.** In the scriptural context, we are often reminded to *"speak the truth in love"* (Ephesians 4:15), which serves as a guiding principle fostering respect amidst disagreement.

Communication: The Channel for Respect

Efficient communication is an indispensable strategy for sustaining respect. **When confronting opposing opinions, listen more than you speak**. Ancient wisdom instructs us to be *"quick to listen, slow to speak"* (James 1:19), and there is profound merit to this advice, particularly in a business context where active listening can lead to more insightful decision-making. **Truly hearing another's perspective without formulating a rebuttal in real-time demands patience and discipline, yet it paves the way for genuine respect and can defuse potential conflict.** This approach reveals a sincere desire to understand, and signals a respect that transcends differences.

The Art of Disagreeing without Disrespect

In moments of divergent viewpoints, remember that **disagreeing does not equate to discounting another's self worth, value or intelligence**. **We must differentiate between the person and his or her perspective.** A potent tool in accomplishing this is the use of "I" statements, which frame our responses in a way that expresses our views without attacking the opposition. By saying, "I understand your point, but I see it differently," we preserve the dignity of the discourse. This reflects not only an emotionally intelligent response but also a key aspect of spiritual maturity – the ability to embrace both grace and truth.

Considerate Confrontation

It's inevitable that sometimes agreement cannot be reached, and there may be a need for firm confrontation. Yet, even in these instances, **we can confront ideas without being confrontational toward the individual**. The mark of a true leader is someone who can assert his or her stance without alienation and who can stand firm in their convictions while remaining open to dialogue. Anchored by both steadfast faith and an understanding of human dynamics, the guidance to *"let your speech always be with grace, seasoned with salt"* (Colossians 4:6), offers a blueprint for effective, respectful communication in every sphere.

Empathy: A Bridge Over Troubled Waters

Fostering respect in disagreement also necessitates empathy. **Taking the time to consider the experiences and emotions that shape someone's viewpoint can transform a potential debate into a moment of connection.** In the world of entrepreneurship, where divergent thoughts can lead to innovation and growth, harnessing empathy is an asset. Rather than simply tolerating varying insights, empathetic engagement allows us to value them as contributions to a richer, more nuanced understanding of the challenges at hand.

Conflict as Opportunity for Growth

When met with resistance, we might feel like retreating or doubling down. Yet here lies an opportunity for both personal and professional growth. Conflict, when approached with respect and humility, can be an engine for improvement. The respected spiritual principle of *"iron sharpens iron"* (Proverbs 27:17) is pertinent in these scenarios – through the friction of conflicting opinions, we can refine our ideas and our approach, sharpening our intellect and enhancing our interactions. In a boardroom, this principle can drive innovation and propel the company forward, as diverse perspectives are not only heard but are also used to challenge and improve upon the status quo.

Solidifying Bonds Beyond Business

Maintaining respect despite differences has the power to strengthen relationships in ways that transcend the immediate context. The skills honed in the course of diplomatic disagreements transfer into all arenas of life, solidifying bonds with those around us. **When we navigate discussions with respect, others are more inclined to reciprocate, creating a virtuous cycle. By leading by example, we can influence the culture of our workplaces and communities, cultivating a climate where robust, respectful debate is the norm, and where individuals feel valued, heard, and empowered to contribute their unique insights and perspectives.**

At the heart of every meaningful conversation is the ability to see beyond our own reflections in the opinions of others. It's a noble pursuit to seek understanding rather than simply validation from our exchanges. One of the most transformative shifts we can make is to decouple our sense of personal value from the requirement of shared perspectives. This is not just a strategy for harmony, but a foundational principle for engaging with grace even when under fire.

Navigating discussions with individuals who hold opposing views can be likened to steering a course through uncharted waters. Uncertainty often gives rise to anxiety, but the true navigator is one who captains their ship with poise, irrespective of the tumultuous seas. **Spiritual wisdom encourages us to be steadfast in love and patient in conflict**; drawing upon such teachings enables us to remain anchored in respect, even amidst the storm of disagreement.

Embodying Respect in Every Interaction

In the professional realm, just as in personal spheres, the caliber of our relationships is not gauged merely by the agreements we share, but by the respect that underpins our interactions. When we enter a boardroom or negotiation table, we bring with us a commitment to honor the human dignity of our counterparts. It's important to display a level of civility and decorum that transcends the immediate transaction. As stewards of integrity, we model a standard of discourse that can shape our culture for the better.

To be effective and respected communicators, we must not only articulate our views with clarity but also listen actively to the narratives of others. In doing so, we forge a bridge of mutual understanding. Personal anecdotes serve as powerful tools in this endeavor — they are threads that weave together the tapestry of a broader, collective story. Engaging through narrative allows us to contextualize differing opinions, providing a pathway to empathy instead of escalation.

Facilitating Grace Under Pressure

Consider the scenario in which a work colleague or a classmate vehemently disagrees with your proposal. Here, the immediate response is not to counter-attack but to pause and seek insight. Why does their perspective differ? What experiences may have shaped their viewpoint? Approach the divergence as an opportunity to expand your understanding, rather than a battleground to defend your position.

The most influential leaders and thinkers across time have been those who possessed the rare ability to extricate their sense of self-worth from the arena of ideas. They engaged in debates with fervor yet retained a sense of humility and graciousness that elevated the discourse. We need only look at historical figures from Nelson Mandela to Abraham Lincoln, who, though steadfast in their convictions, extended respect to their dissenters.

Harnessing the Power of Diverse Thought

In a world increasing in complexity and intertwined fate, appreciating the wealth that lies in diverse thought is not only wise, it's vital. Economics, politics, and theology all teach us that systems thrive on varied inputs and perspectives. When we internalize the understanding that our personal value is not diminished by the plurality of voices, we enable a symphony of ideas to rise—a symphony richer than any singular melody.

In business and entrepreneurship, this principle is immensely practical. Encouraging an environment where employees feel valued enough to dissent without fear of retribution leads to innovation and growth. Every thriving enterprise is a testament to the power of collective intellect, where respect is the currency that fuels forward momentum.

Persevering Through Challenging Dialogues

The pursuit of harmony in discourse is a testament to our belief in the potential for growth, both personal and communal. By demonstrating respect amidst disagreement, we pave the way for a more collaborative and connected society. Moreover, **we offer ourselves the opportunity to evolve, to refine our thoughts, and perhaps even to change our minds. This is not an admission of weakness but an act of intellectual and spiritual maturity.**

The strategies outlined in this discussion are not theoretical niceties; they are actionable truths. They demand of us a courageous heart and a clear mind. It takes practice and intentionality, but the rewards are self-evident. Employ these principles not only as tactics for survival in a polarized world but as cornerstones for building bridges where walls once stood. It is here, in the crucible of conflicting ideas, that we discover our capacity for growth, resilience, and, ultimately, respect that reaches beyond the superficial harmony of mere agreement.

The Strength of the Individual Unbound by Uniformity

As leaders, entrepreneurs, and influencers, we must decouple personal value from shared perspectives. The ability to do so is akin to a tree firmly rooted in the soil of self-assurance — able to withstand the winds of differing opinions without being uprooted. We stand strong, not because everyone echoes our thoughts, but because we recognize the intrinsic worth of each person and each unique viewpoint.

Let us not forget that our value does not diminish because of dissent. Quite the contrary, our value is enriched by our willingness to engage with varied perspectives, to learn, to adapt, and to grow. It is a beautiful process, reminiscent of the biblical 'iron *sharpening iron*', allowing us to shape and be shaped through the exchange of ideas. How we handle discord can become a testament to our personal growth, emotional maturity and professionalism.

The Power of Civil Discourse in the Professional Sphere

In a professional context, it is especially critical to uphold respect in the face of disagreement, for it sets the stage for innovation and progress. Practical experience confirms that some of the most successful business ventures have stemmed from leaders who did not shy away from diverse thoughts but rather welcomed them as fuel for creative solutions.

Actionable advice? **When facing dissent, listen not only to what is being said but also understand the underlying concerns and motivations.** This enables you to engage more effectively, finding common ground even when the ground seems to fracture. It's not simply about being correct, but about being wise and compassionate in our interactions.

Let us be motivated to act, inspired by the wisdom of myriad spiritual, political, and economic voices which have, throughout history, found strength in diversity. Embrace this richness in thought, allow it to inform our interactions, and let's move forward with a renewed commitment to **deepen connections** in a world too often divided.

3

THE INTELLECTUAL EVOLUTION

In the midst of the bustling city, where steel met sky and ambition intertwined with the stars, there walked Jacob, his thoughts as crowded as the sidewalk he navigated. Amid the murmur of commerce and the symphony of honking horns, he grappled with a recent boardroom confrontation — a test of his resolve and beliefs about the path of his young tech company.

The office, cast in the amber glow of morning light, was a battleground of ideas, and Jacob's pivot from the company's original strategy had sparked much controversy. As autumn leaves danced whimsically to the ground, Jacob's mind, too, pirouetted between confidence and doubt. Once firm in conviction, new data whispered a contrary tale, urging adaptation. Such flexibility, he learned from spiritual teachings that valued humility, was not a frailty but wisdom manifest — a mark of the intellectually honest and agile entrepreneur.

Like the midday sun clarifies the hues of the city, a passage from Proverbs echoed in his heart: *"Plans fail for lack of counsel, but with many advisers they succeed."* The clash of perspectives was not turmoil but counsel, a crucible forging a new, wiser direction. Jacob's steps, reflecting this internal shift, moved with renewed purpose.

As he walked, his pocket buzzed — a call from his mentor. Pulling the phone from his suit, his heart swelled with the kind of warmth felt in conversation with a trusted friend. The mentor, with decades of executive experience, held entrepreneurial battlescars of his own, yet he always urged Jacob towards perseverance and faith in the ever-unfolding journey. Their dialogue was less a lecture, more a mutual exchange of insights steeped in respect and camaraderie.

With the close of the call, Jacob's stride slowed before a small park where the harmonies of a solitary saxophonist filled the air. The city seemed to hold its breath, and in this rare moment of tranquility, Jacob found clarity. Real-world examples from his mentor affirmed the virtue in evolving one's mindset. To change one's mind was to pilot one's venture with precision and care, attuned to the winds of change.

The day waned, yet the entrepreneur's spirit did not; finding comfort in the fluidity of business, akin to the teachings of King Solomon, who knew wisdom was a pursuit, not a possession. It was with this collective wisdom, from across disciplines, that Jacob would reshape his vision, steering his enterprise through uncertain seas towards a brighter dawn.

But could the very act of changing one's mind be the compass that guides us to uncharted territories of success and innovation?

The Courage to Embrace Change

Shifts in our beliefs do not signify the frailty of our character but illuminate the stretches of our intellect. In a landscape often marred by dogmatism, the willingness to alter one's perspective is not merely a testament to humility but a badge of honor, representing intellectual dexterity and honesty. The capacity to accept new ideas and knowledge is indicative of astute discernment, integral to the discourse that shapes our society and our very beings.

The adaptability of our understanding, grounded in the principle of perpetual intellectual growth, aligns with seeking greater truths and a higher moral compass. It is in this transformative process that we are often closest to the divine wisdom that many seek.

The business world, too, reserves its applause for those who boldly stride through the evolving marketplace with a growth mindset. They champion adaptability as the cornerstone of progress and enterprise. It is an entrepreneurial spirit that respects not the altar of the status quo but the crucible of innovation — a directive that calls on every individual to pursue their goals with an acceptance that the path may change as knowledge and circumstances evolve.

From a wealth of real-world experiences, we understand the pitfalls of a stagnant mentality. **The companies and individuals who lead industries are often those who have mastered the art of iteration, consistently refining their ideas and products in light of feedback and new data**. This chapter, therefore, insists on **the merit of a mind open to revision, considering such flexibility not as vacillation but as a strategic and deliberate advancement towards excellence.**

In fostering open-mindedness, we acknowledge that intellectual honesty is a compass that can guide us through tumultuous debates and discussions. To value flexibility is not to waver aimlessly but to navigate thoughtfully through complex issues, ever ready to steer our minds toward truths that had eluded us before. Celebrating an evolving thought process becomes integral to learning, which in itself is a lifelong enterprise, springing from the very fabric of our quest for meaning and understanding.

We live in an era where ideas are the currency of progress, and diversity of thought is both the challenge and the solution to intractable problems. Fostering an environment that esteems the fluidity of thought and the courage to change one's mind encourages constructive dissent, the kind from which the harmony of truly progressive solutions can emerge. As we engage in the endeavor of continual learning, let us revel in the process of intellectual evolution as our shared path to enlightenment and societal advancement.

Thusly, encouraging an atmosphere of intellectual growth serves more than personal betterment; it is foundational to the harmony of a forward-thinking, innovative society. **By reconceptualizing the notion of changing one's mind, we open the door to dialogues that spark change, to connections that ignite inspiration, and to an acceptance that the truest form of agreement may indeed dwell in our ability to respect and embrace our intellectual disparities.**

Reconsidering one's position in the face of new information or perspectives is not indicative of a fickle mind but, rather, a sign of intellectual maturity. Historically, some of the most transformative leaders and thinkers — figures who resonate strongly within our spiritual traditions — were those who evolved in their thinking, demonstrating a formative flexibility. Like the Biblical Paul, who once stood against early Christians and became an apostle after a profound encounter with God, arguably the first ever "come to Jesus" moment historically, on the road to Damascus, a change of mind can be a powerful testament to personal growth and a commitment to truth.

The mark of a resilient intellect is not in unwavering rigidity, but in its capacity to absorb new insights and experiences. In the entrepreneurial world, we praise innovators who pivot from failed business strategies to more promising avenues. Just as these business leaders must admit when an approach isn't working, we too must regard intellectual adaptability, similar to course correction for NASA, as a strategic advantage, a necessary component for navigating complex moral and theological debates, economic policies, or political landscapes.

Fostering an environment that respects intellectual growth requires us to shed the stigma of inconsistency. Respected spiritual texts encourage us to seek wisdom constantly; they portray mind-changing not as a shortcoming, but as an admirable endeavor. There is spiritual profundity in admitting that our understanding is incomplete, reminiscent of Socratic teachings that asserted wisdom in recognizing one's own ignorance.

Open-mindedness is not just a buzzword for inclusiveness but a strategic approach to problem-solving. **It is the ability to balance faith with reason, and tradition with innovation.** By embracing intellectual growth, we cultivate leaders who can blend the humility of a learner with the vision of a prophet. This duality is often the bedrock of sound decision-making, particularly in complex business scenarios where foresight is just as valuable as historical knowledge.

To truly value the process of changing one's mind, we must acknowledge the courage it takes to diverge from one's past convictions. Personal anecdotes from respected leaders, who once held opposing views but had the tenacity to pursue truth over tradition, can serve as a potent form of motivation. By sharing such transformative narratives, we not only humanize the intellectual journey but also inspire others to embark on their paths towards enlightenment.

The path to truth is seldom a straight line — it meanders, backtracks, and forges new routes as the landscape of knowledge and understanding evolves. In the rich tapestry of modern discourse, it is important to remember that changing one's mind in the light of new evidence is more than a mere shift in opinion; it is an evolution of consciousness, a step towards greater enlightenment that should not only be forgiven but commended.

The Value of Intellectual Honesty

In an age where information is abundant and opinions are shared with the click of a button, holding fast to intellectual honesty is more than just commendable — it's essential. **Intellectual honesty means having the courage to confront the merits of opposing views and, if necessary, adjust our own.** This is not merely an academic exercise; it extends to every discourse we engage in, from theology to sports. Spiritual texts promote the idea of seeking truth from all sources. The teachings of King Solomon, for example, extol the virtue of listening to understand, rather than to simply respond. In business, this principle dictates that we remain open to innovative ideas, thereby fostering environments where creative solutions blossom. When we **value truth over ego**, we encourage a culture of continuous improvement and integrity.

Embracing Flexibility in Thought

In the pursuit of success, whether personal or professional, flexibility is a critical asset. The ability to adapt to new situations allows us to excel in diverse environments, both in terms of career and personal development. Similarly, embracing intellectual flexibility can lead to breakthroughs in policy-making, where multiple viewpoints often lead to more balanced outcomes. The adept entrepreneur knows this well, always ready to pivot strategy in light of new data or market trends. Thus, valuing flexibility is about more than embracing change; it's about acknowledging that adaptability is a cornerstone of resilience and success.

Encouraging Diverse Discourse

To engage meaningfully with the world and its myriad perspectives, we must champion environments where diverse discourse is not only accepted but encouraged. **This means inviting voices from different disciplines, cultures, and beliefs to the table, recognizing that wisdom can be found in the multitude of counsel.**

Reflect on famed roundtables of history, where the amalgamation of minds from various fields sparked some of the greatest advancements in thought and policy. I think of President Abraham Lincoln's cabinet that included not yes-men but a collection of rivals that challenged his thinking in order to produce the best possible actions for America during a crucial time in history. Creating such a collaborative atmosphere requires respect for the dialogue process, an acceptance that our understanding is always evolving and that today's dissent could be tomorrow's breakthrough.

The Impact of Open-Mindedness on Community

Open-mindedness in our communities is akin to opening the windows of a stuffy room to let the fresh air in. It revitalizes discussions, clears the haze of stubborn prejudice, and brings clarity to collective thought. Our communities, be they spiritual congregations, political strategy roundtables, school classrooms or business networks, thrive when individuals approach discussions with a willingness to listen and learn. It is this spirit that ignites innovation and collaborative strength, building a foundation for collective achievements and shared triumphs. An open mind is akin to fertile soil; it nurtures the seeds of new ideas that can bloom into vibrant contributions to society.

The Continuous Journey of Learning

The journey of learning doesn't have a definitive end; it's a continuous pathway that enriches our lives. Like a good mentor, life presents us with a succession of lessons that, if heeded, hone our discernment and understanding. **It's what keeps the seasoned executive astute, the wise elder insightful, and the shrewd politician effective**. In every facet of life, there's room for growth and improvement. The history of scientific discovery, for instance, is filled with tales of continued learning, where **yesterday's science fiction became today's technology**. So too should our learning process be — a never-ending quest for knowledge and wisdom.

Connecting Through Compromise

The act of finding common ground — where seemingly disparate views find points of agreement — can often lead not just to compromise, but also to surprising innovation. Compromise doesn't mean sacrificing one's principles; rather, it involves locating the bridge between positions. Businesses understand this when they form partnerships, blending different practices for a common venture. Such alliances can lead to unprecedented success, illustrating the power of collaborative agility.

Leadership and Openness to Change

Leaders, be they in boardrooms or on public stages, serve as exemplars of the principles they advocate. Leadership demands an openness to change, an embracing of the evolving nature of the world. This doesn't imply fickleness; rather, it's an acknowledgment of the complexity of our ever-changing global landscape. Spiritual teachings often highlight the necessity of wise leadership — those who guide not only with strength but also with humility to alter course when warranted. In a business sense, it's about being strategically astute while staying responsive to the changing tides of the marketplace. Leaders who embody this blend of steadfastness and adaptability inspire confidence and pave the way for enduring legacies.

Conclusion

Cultivating an attitude of open-mindedness, valuing intellectual honesty, and fostering flexibility are not just philosophical musings — they are the bedrock of successful interpersonal relationships, effective leadership, and innovative organizations. These attributes align with spiritual principles that transcend cultural and religious boundaries, reinforcing the notion that, at our core, we seek understanding and truth. They provide a compass in navigating the complexities of social dynamics, political landscapes, and economic challenges.

As you engage with the ideas presented here, consider not only their implications for intellectual evolution, but also their transformative potential in the practical realm of everyday interactions and decision-making. This isn't simply about changing minds; it's about enriching them with the depth and breadth of human knowledge and experience.

Take action, reflect on your core beliefs and be prepared to adjust them in the light of new evidence, for this is the hallmark of a life lived in passionate pursuit of knowledge. Arm yourself with an open mind, for it is the most powerful tool in your arsenal, whether you are navigating growth prospects at a start-up, mediating conflicts around the dinner table, or engaging in the marketplace of ideas at your town hall.

Persist and persevere on this path, and forge ahead with the confidence that comes from knowing that the capacity to change one's mind is far from a liability—it is one of the greatest assets a thinker can possess. This ability will distinguish you as a leader, a visionary, and a true intellectual.

In the end, it is not simply about winning arguments or amassing facts. It is about fostering a world where diversity of thought is not just heard but heeded, a world where enlightenment is not a finite point but a boundless journey. As we continue to engage with the vibrant tapestry of human opinion and experience, let us be ever-mindful that growth — intellectual, personal, and spiritual — remains an infinite pursuit, worthy of our deepest respect and most earnest endeavors.

4

— ❦ —

BIAS BARRIERS AND DEBATE BRIDGES

In the sober light of the boardroom, Martin, with his eyes tracing the grain of the polished oak table, contemplated the forthcoming diversity training workshop. Clasping the cold steel of his pen, he couldn't shake the nagging twinge of skepticism. "What if," he mused, "we become so caught up in this maze of biases that every word becomes a step through a minefield?" A world-worn bible laid resolutely on his desk at home, its passages on humility whispering at the edge of his consciousness.

Trees swayed gently outside, their dance observed through floor-to-ceiling windows that bordered the sterile room. The sway of greenery, a testament to the winds of change that had consistently buffeted his company's sails. Martin was a captain of industry, yet now he felt a subtle trepidation in his belly — was it not the same feeling Noah might've had as he hammered the last plank of the ark, trusting in a purpose greater than himself?

The very mention of cognitive biases, which the upcoming training aimed to dismantle, caused his executive team to shuffle papers or clear their throats. Confirmation bias, they would learn, was a form of mental errancy, a barrier to the fruitful amalgamation of diverse perspectives. Martin knew the scriptures valued a multitude of counselors, but how could he transpose such ancient wisdom into the modern market's relentless tempo?

As he leaned back in his chair, the city's hum reached his ears, a symphony of progress and a reminder of the resilience embedded in his company's ethos. To persevere, to innovate — these were the mantras that had carried them from a modest startup to a juggernaut in their field. Yet, in the spirit of entrepreneurs who understood that success lay not only in profitable numbers but in the cultivation of good character, Martin whispered a silent prayer for guidance.

The rustle of a colleague snapping her laptop shut interrupted his reverie. She, too, knew the weight of change, the burden of intro-spection. Their eyes met, and without words they shared a moment of silent agreement. To be open to learning was to acknowledge the finite nature of one's human understanding. Surely wisdom could be found in the convergence of life experience and the humility to accept new truths?

As the meeting adjourned, Martin's thoughts lingered on the edge of unease and anticipation. Perhaps this training would be a crucible, one that would test and refine their corporate ethos. The early evening light cast long shadows across the room as they all filed out, their silhouettes like prophets of a future unwritten.

How might embracing these cognitive challenges reshape the way we understand our businesses, ourselves, and the very fabric of society?

The Invisible Walls We Build

The act of conversation is akin to weaving a tapestry, with threads of personal history, knowledge, and opinion intertwining to form a complex picture of collective human understanding. Yet, often un-beknownst to us, certain threads — cognitive biases — tangle this process, pulling us further from harmony. In the realms of business and personal growth, these biases are like barriers to insight, preventing us from seeing the full spectrum of potential and opportunity. As we navigate discussions in an increasingly polarized society, identifying these invisible walls becomes paramount to fostering connections that transcend mere tolerance, reaching the zenith of true collaboration and innovation.

Awareness is the first step towards transformation. In business and in life, recognizing the biases that color our perceptions and conversations is an act of mental discipline, akin to the mindfulness found in spiritual teachings. As we search for truths within our dialogues, it's vital to understand how often we are unknowingly selective in processing information. Reflecting upon the sacred texts that encourage seekers to approach others with a humble heart, we are reminded to bring this humility to every interaction, **acknowledging our limited human perspective and the possibility of revelation through others.**

Central to our journey of embracing diversity of thought is the ongoing commitment to personal development. **The pursuit of dialogue as an art form requires persistence, a willingness to remain open, and a readiness to unlearn as much as learn**. From the boardroom to the community meeting, techniques that mitigate prejudice are not merely ethical obligations but strategic imperatives. They evolve our discourse from competitive clashes to a symphony of ideas where each voice is heard and valued.

In cultivating a growth mindset open to learning, we echo the spiritual pursuit of enlightenment, where **each soul is both teacher and student**. Regardless of our preconceptions, embracing varied perspectives is an act of faith in humanity's collective wisdom. **It demands that we listen — not only to respond but to understand.**

This devotional approach to dialogue mirrors the humility and respect taught by the wise, translating it into our daily interactions.

Yet, understanding biases is not purely an academic exercise — it requires real-world application. Anecdotes of transformative conversations, where individuals surmounted their biases to achieve common goals, offer practical evidence of the power within our grasp. Business leaders, policy-makers, and community champions have long discovered that the greatest breakthroughs stem from diverse coalitions forged in mutual respect and curiosity.

Navigating through our own cognitive labyrinths, we find strategies that guide us out of the shadows of ignorance and into the light of awareness. By embracing these strategies, we generate not only success in our ventures but also deeper connections with those around us. **Imagine a professional work environment where varied opinions are not threats but assets**, where dissent is not a discordant note but the very harmony that enriches the music of progress.

In this vein, may we approach each conversation with the resolve to offer our insights freely and receive wisdom gratefully, establishing a foundation for unity in a world too often fragmented by unchallenged biases. As we break down these unseen barriers within ourselves, we begin to construct bridges of understanding that can span the greatest divides — a testament to the enduring spirit of human collaboration and the boundless potential when minds and hearts align in pursuit of shared visions.

Understanding our cognitive predispositions is akin to clearing the fog from a landscape, revealing the intricate details that were previously obscured. In the realm of meaningful conversations, cognitive biases stand as subtle yet formidable barriers to clear communication and understanding. These biases are the silent gatekeepers of our comfort zones, often preventing us from fully appreciating the variety of perspectives that surround us.

The **confirmation bias**, for example, is a common cognitive filter that **selectively absorbs information conforming to our existing beliefs while deflecting contradictory evidence**. It's a mental shortcut that whispers reassurance but also constructs a fortress around our opinions, **often causing intellectual stagnation**. Recognizing this bias within ourselves is the first step toward constructing bridges over the chasms that divide us during discussions.

Another subtle intruder in our dialogues is the **availability heuristic** — our tendency to overweigh the significance of information that comes to mind quickly and easily. This can be the news story we just watched or an anecdote shared by a friend. **Often, it is not the most accurate or relevant data that shapes our viewpoints, but rather the most recent or memorable**. To converse effectively and fairly, we must be willing to question the representativeness of the evidence we conveniently recall.

Digging deeper into our mental toolkit, we uncover the **anchoring bias — our inclination to heavily rely on the first piece of information we hear**. When discussing any subject, the initial argument presented can unduly sway our understanding and subsequent arguments. It is our responsibility to acknowledge this proclivity and strive to evaluate new information with fresh eyes, thus ensuring a more balanced and holistic view.

The **actor-observer bias** nudges us toward a double standard, **where we attribute our own actions to external circumstances while judging others' actions as reflections of their character**. This bias can sour conversations as it leads to misunderstandings and unfair assessments of others' motivations and actions. By practicing empathy and extending the benefit of the doubt to our conversation partners, we counter this bias effectively.

Joining the list of culprits, the **self-serving bias stokes the flames of self-righteousness, encouraging us to attribute successes to our own efforts and failures to external factors**. This outlook can lead to conversations fraught with self-justifications rather than collaborative problem-solving. Recognizing and tempering this bias can help us approach conversations with humility and openness to learning.

Moving forward, let us take these insights as tools for transformation. The journey to becoming adept in the art of conversation is marked by recognition, adjustment, and continual learning. Our next step involves developing techniques to mitigate bias and engage in dialogues with the grace of humility.

Recognizing Our Limitations

As evident in many spiritual texts, humility stands as a profound virtue from which learning and growth can spring. To effectively engage in dialogue that bridges gaps and breaks bias barriers, we must first recognize our own limitations. Accepting that we do not possess all knowledge and that our perspective is but one amongst a multitude, requires a humility that can be deeply challenging yet incredibly freeing. **Like a scholar who approaches a vast library with both awe and the realization of their limited understanding, we should enter conversations with an openness to the wealth of knowledge others hold.** Embrace the discomfort of not always having the answers, for it is in this space that authentic dialogue can flourish.

Active Listening as a Pathway to Understanding

Active listening is a critical skill in mitigating bias and engaging humbly in discussions. **It is the art of fully concentrating on the speaker without the distraction of formulating a response or silently critiquing his or her viewpoint.** It involves giving him or her your full attention, nodding in acknowledgement, and providing feedback that confirms his or her message has been heard and considered. To master active listening, consider the Biblical call to be *"quick to listen, slow to speak, and slow to anger"* (James 1:19). When we truly listen, we validate the other person's experiences and create space for mutual understanding. Imagine a family scenario where instead of interrupting or waiting for a gap to affirm your point, you allow your spouse or child to articulate his or her ideas completely. This practice not only fosters respect but often illuminates perspectives we had not considered, ultimately leading to more informed decision-making.

The Power of Questions

Inquisitiveness is a strategic tool in overcoming one's own cognitive biases. **Being genuinely curious about another person's perspective is a hallmark of a mindset aiming to bridge the divide between one another. By asking thoughtful questions, we communicate a genuine interest in the speaker's beliefs and reasons behind them.** It is an expression of humility, in a nod to the concept popularized by the late great Dr. Stephen Covey, that we seek to understand others before we seek to be understood by them. Phrasing matters; **questions should be open-ended and non-threatening, inviting an exchange of ideas rather than an interrogation.** In the political realm, for instance, transformative policies have often been the result of such inquisitive approaches, where solutions evolve from a dialogue that starts with curiosity rather than conflict.

Suspending Immediate Judgment

The initial impulse to judge is a common human reaction; however, suspending this judgment is essential for honest and bias-free discussions. Acknowledging our knee-jerk and often emotional reactions and then setting them aside prepares the ground for more constructive dialogue. A testament to this practice can be seen in mediation settings, where parties are encouraged to listen to opposing perspectives without immediately ascribing them right or wrong. As business leaders or entrepreneurs, adopting a similar stance opens doors for innovation and collaboration that might remain shut under the weight of premature judgment or prejudice.

Fostering Empathy Through Personal Connection

Empathy is the compelling force that can drive us beyond our preconceptions and towards a more profound understanding of others. Personal anecdotes can effectively bridge emotional gaps, appealing to our innate capacity for compassion. **Sharing stories and personal experiences is not only cathartic but also serves as a potent reminder that behind every belief is a human being with emotions, dreams, and struggles.** Whether in the classroom or in town hall meetings, when stories resonate with our own, empathy blossoms, and biases begin to lose their stronghold.

The Art of Conceding Points

One of the most humble acts in a dialogue is the willingness to concede a point. Admitting that another's argument holds merit demonstrates an openness to learning and a flexibility of thought foundational for constructive conversations. This is not to suggest that one should abandon their convictions, but rather, to acknowledge the complexity of issues and the validity of multiple perspectives. It mirrors the wisdom found in Proverbs, which encourages us to listen to advice and accept instruction, so we may gain wisdom in the future (Proverbs 19:20). In a business setting, this approach can lead to more collaborative decision-making processes and more nimble market responses, while it can also avoid the entrenchment that comes with unyielding stances or doubling down on ineffective strategies.

Continuous Self-Reflection

To engage with others effectively, frequent self-reflection is invaluable. **Assessing our thought patterns, questioning our assumptions, and scrutinizing our motives can help to unearth the biases that filter our understanding**. Self-reflection is a journey that parallels the pursuit of knowledge and ethical conduct extolled in spiritual life. In the entrepreneurial world, such introspection can reveal blind spots that hinder growth and innovation, paving the way for more enlightened leadership.

By adopting these techniques, we equip ourselves to overcome the barriers of bias and foster dialogue infused with humility and respect. The act of learning from others, regardless of our own preconceptions, is not only a pathway to greater understanding but also a testament to the celebration of diversity of thought. It is through this enlightened engagement that we can transform potential conflicts into meaningful connections, leading to personal growth and collective progress.

Taking Small Steps Toward Big Change

Begin by making small, conscious efforts to suspend judgment and truly listen during your next discussion. **Even when disagreements arise, focus on the underlying concerns rather than the heated emotions.** By advocating fairness and equanimity, you not only demonstrate leadership but also encourage others to follow suit. Combine this with the spiritual principle of doing unto others as you would have them do unto you, and you create a fertile ground for mutual respect and shared progress.

By integrating these practices into our daily conversations, we not only enhance our personal and professional interactions but also contribute to a larger cultural shift towards deeper understanding and cooperation. In a world that often seems divided, let us be the agents of unity, fostering environments where diverse thoughts can harmonize and collective wisdom can flourish.

The Path Ahead: From Understanding to Action

In our pursuit of unity amidst diversity, actionable steps can transform understanding into lived experience. Begin by observing your conversations. Identify instances where bias creeps in, and actively counteract these tendencies. Engage in dialogues, not as adversaries, but as companions on a shared journey of growth and discovery. Let us all, from all walks of life in the home, the boardroom, the classroom, the political debate, and the community place of worship, step forward with a commitment to breaking down the barriers that bias erects, and in doing so, building bridges that connect us all in meaningful ways.

5

THE ALCHEMY OF LOGIC AND EMPATHY

In the gentle hum of a late afternoon, Elizabeth sat at her polished mahogany desk. The sunlight slanted through the blinds, casting striped shadows that danced across the financial reports and strategic plans strewn before her. The office around her bustled with a quiet efficiency, the scent of ink and ambition intermingling in the air.

She held a pen, a slender silver conduit of thought to paper, but her mind was not on the numbers that dictated the success of her enterprise. Instead, it delved into the recent board meeting, an affair that had been as much about the spirit as it was about strategy. Her reflections were interrupted by the soft chime of the antique clock on the wall, a reminder of the passing time and the decisions that awaited her.

In that room of commerce, no scripture lay open, yet Elizabeth's decisions were guided by a faith deeper than balance sheets. She remembered the words of Proverbs 15:22, *"Plans fail for lack of counsel, but with many advisers they succeed."* The advice she sought was not only in ledgers, but in the hearts of her colleagues, the very souls bound up in the collective journey of their business.

Her mind circled back to the empathy she had offered and received in the course of challenging dialogues. The meeting had been a practiced dance between caution and boldness, each executive at the table bringing their own deeply held beliefs and emotions into the conversation. To balance these perspectives with the incisive edge of reason was her art, and the canvas was the future they crafted together.

As the day waned, Elizabeth stood, stretching the stiffness from her limbs as she walked to the window. She regarded the sprawling city below, each building a testament to the principles of logic and engineering, yet each window a glimpse into the lives driven by emotion and experience. Such was the duality that defined leadership in the modern age, where the vigor of commerce met the gentleness of human connection.

She contemplated her next steps, each one a potential parable of perseverance for budding entrepreneurs who would one day walk these halls. She thought of those she mentored, the bright-eyed youth seeking to navigate the labyrinth of industry with compasses of intellect and empathy.

Could they perceive the delicate balance required to thrive amidst the cacophony of the marketplace? Would they learn, as she had, that the wisdom to listen often outweighs the desire to speak? And in the silence that cloaks decision, might they find that the true measure of success lies not only in profit, but in the ability to harmonize the head with the heart?

When Rationality Meets Compassion

In a world brimming with clashing convictions, the quest for civil discourse seems like an elusive alchemy, struggling to meld the rigid precision of logic with the soft contours of empathy. Yet, it's within this challenging fusion that the secret to harmonious discussion lies. This harmonization is not merely an idealistic, feel-good aspiration but a pragmatic approach that elevates our conversations to be more inclusive, insightful, and transformative. **The essence of civil debate has evolved beyond the mere exchange of ideas; it now requires a tapestry woven with the threads of emotional intelligence and intellectual rigor.**

The art of balancing heart and mind speaks directly to the core of human interaction. Think of logic as the skeleton that provides structure to an argument, while empathy acts as the muscle that allows it to move and adapt. Stripped of either, our discourse becomes either a brittle construct, easily shattered by the weight of disagreement, or an amorphous entity, incapable of holding its shape. Combining these elements is not an effortless task, but it's through their integration that we can elevate the standards of how we engage with differing viewpoints, especially within the often fractious realms of politics, religion, and social issues.

Recognizing the importance of empathy in logical debate isn't tantamount to surrendering to pure emotion; rather, it acknowledges that the human experience and the persuasion it fosters are inherently emotional in nature. **A debate devoid of empathy risks not only alienating the opposition but also overlooking key aspects of the human condition that can provide critical context to the dialogue**. By balancing empathetic understanding with intellectual strength, one is not diluting the argument, but enriching it, allowing the discourse to reach beyond the superficial layers of contention, touching the more profound strata of collective human experience.

Developing a nuanced approach to discussions where the head and the heart are valued equally can be a transformative experience. It's about transcending ego, recognizing the inherent worth in each person's perspective, and understanding that diversity of thought, when approached with respect and consideration, can be the cornerstone of collective growth. It's an approach that speaks to the entrepreneurial spirit, the one that seeks to innovate and connect, to build bridges where divides once existed.

The Delicate Dance of Discerning Debates

Embarking on the journey towards thoughtful debate is not a voyage of whims; rather, it requires careful preparation and a discernible goal in mind. **Define your objective clearly**; is this debate a pathway to broaden your horizon or a stage to articulate your convictions and win over your audience? Your clarity in purpose will be the compass that guides your engagement, ensuring that every argument made is a step forward in your quest, not a mere echo in the chamber of discord.

The Debate Conductor's Blueprint

Research both sides thoroughly. A judicious debater is akin to a maestro, intimately familiar with every note and nuance of the composition. You must delve deeply into the symphony of perspectives, understanding each argument's crescendos and diminuendos. With robust knowledge comes the capacity to anticipate counterpoints and engage in a discourse that is both comprehensive and profound.

Awareness of one's inclinations and preferences is crucial. Before stepping onto the debate floor, **analyze your own biases**. Just like a beam of light passing through a prism is refracted, so too are our perceptions colored by the spectrum of our experiences and prejudices. Recognizing this subjectivity allows us to approach discussions with humility and openness, laying the groundwork for a genuine and respectful exchange of ideas.

Develop strong arguments; not the ones that merely resonate in echo chambers or when you "preach to the choir", but those that withstand the scrutiny of opposition. The strength of your argument is measured not by its volume but by its validity and the evidence that supports it. As you craft your argument, make each word count, each fact relevant, and each point a brick in the foundation of your thesis.

Anticipation is the mark of a seasoned debater. **Anticipate counterarguments** like a chess grandmaster foresees moves on the board. Formulate responses that show your engagement with the opposition's perspective, demonstrating an understanding that is both analytical and empathetic.

The soul of debate lies in the exchange; thus, **practice active listening** with the fervor of a student seeking wisdom from its teacher. Listening is as much about hearing the words as it is about comprehending the intent behind them. It's about respect, patience, and the willingness to find common ground. Through active listening emerges the potential for productive dialogue and the transformation of conflict into connection.

Your demeanor, including your tone and body language, often speaks louder than your actual words. A debate charged with unchecked emotion is like a vessel adrift in a tempest. **Keep emotions in check** to navigate through the rough waters of dissent. Emotional regulation does not imply impassivity; it means maintaining a demeanor of calm and respect that enables constructive conversation.

By adhering to this blueprint, you set the stage for not just a debate, but a conduit for understanding and learning in the marketplace of ideas — a forum where opposing positions can be shared and examined with both intellectual rigor and a compassionate spirit. This is the synthesis that transforms adversaries into allies, and it is this synthesis that is essential for moving forward in a polarized world.

The crux of any meaningful conversation hinges on a simple, yet profound, synergy: the marriage of logic and empathy. In the arena of civil discourse, this union becomes particularly crucial. It's about grounding our interactions in reasoned debate while acknowledging the emotional human experience. Indeed, balanced discourse hinges on the ability to dissect a problem with intellectual precision yet also embrace the emotions and perspectives that give valuable context to the issue at hand.

Spiritual teachings across traditions have long maintained the virtue of empathy; consider the biblical "Golden Rule" (Matthew 7:12), which advocates treating others as one wishes to be treated. Such profound spiritual teachings remind us that empathy is not merely a sentiment but a mindset that when combined with reason, leads to more humane and constructive discourse.

In the business world, we talk a lot about the importance of "soft skills" and emotional intelligence, and empathy is at the forefront of both. However, empathy should not be mistaken for a lack of rigor. On the contrary, **empathy is the lubricant that allows the gears of logic and reason to turn without grating**. It is an entrepreneurial imperative to engage different viewpoints with a respectful understanding, as this lays the foundation for innovative solutions that resonate on a deeper human level.

From my experience, I have observed that the most adept negotiators are those who balance analytical prowess with a keen sense of emotional intelligence. They know when to press a point and when to step back and appreciate the other's stance. It is this balancing act — this alchemy of logic and empathy — that turns a potentially adversarial conversation into a collaborative search for understanding and resolution.

The wisdom of integrating insights from various fields stands pertinent here. Political science teaches us the structure of argumentation, while psychology offers us insights into human behavior. Economics, with its focus on costs and benefits, encourages us to weigh the pragmatic and financial consequences and tradeoffs of actions and policies. When we draw upon these disparate but essential strands of knowledge, we fortify our capacity for reasoned empathy.

Let's take a moment to envision discussing a contentious issue. Picture the scenario, not as a confrontation, but as an opportunity for connection. Sharing personal anecdotes can help convey the challenges of entwining logic with empathy while still reaching effective conclusions. By doing so, we transfer the abstract into the tangible, ensuring our dialogue transcends mere theory and takes on the warmth of shared human experience.

Approaching issues with a teacher's enthusiasm, we find that even complex topics become accessible. We are the guides navigating through the nuances of discourse, inviting others to understand the depth of our convictions while remaining open to the depth of theirs, showcasing the paramount importance of being not only intelligent but also intentional in our approach to conversations.

The Interplay of Intellect and Emotion

In the realm of civil discourse, the infusion of intellectual rigor with emotional acuity is akin to the blending of steel and silk; each contributes unique strengths to the ensemble, making the whole more resilient and adaptable. **A logical argument brings structure and clarity, while empathy infuses the debate with warmth and un-**

derstanding. Together, they create a dialogue that is not only cogent but also compassionate, reaching hearts as well as minds. As Proverbs 15:1 teaches us, *"A gentle answer turns away wrath, but a harsh word stirs up anger."* This tenet underscores the necessity of tempering truth with tenderness in our conversations.

Balancing intellectual rigor with sensitivity requires a careful dance. We can still employ sharp analytics without compromising empathy. Through active listening and acknowledging the emotions and viewpoints of others, we are not diluting our logic. Instead, we engage on a multifaceted level that **respects both the content and the context of the discourse**. This dual approach aligns closely with the teachings of the Apostle Paul, who in Ephesians 4:15, urges us to **speak the truth in love**. The pursuit here is not merely to win an argument but to foster understanding and connection.

Emotions as Helpful Data Points

Perceiving emotions as data points in a debate allows for a more holistic understanding of the issue at hand. Emotions are not distractions; they are indicators of deeply held values and concerns that can inform our logical analysis. We must remember the wisdom of Ecclesiastes 7:9, *"Do not be quickly provoked in your spirit, for anger resides in the lap of fools."* By considering others' feelings as worthy of analysis, we avoid the folly of callously dismissing critical aspects of human experience which could otherwise provide valuable insights into the broader conversation.

Tools for Thoughtful Engagement

Business leaders often understand that managing a team requires both a strategic and a personal touch. The same principle applies to dialogue. Developing a practical toolbox for intellectual and empathetic engagement is critical. This includes active listening skills, emotional intelligence training, and techniques for navigating conflict deftly. These tools not only allow us to dissect arguments but also provide the means to maintain civil relationships in the face of disagreement.

Leading with Empathy

When opening a dialogue, lead with empathy. This doesn't mean sacrificing your point of view but rather setting a table where all ideas can be consumed with respect. **Imagine walking into a negotiation; your counterpart expects a hard sell, yet you start by genuinely inquiring about their needs and fears. This unexpected approach often disarms and opens a channel for more productive conversations**, echoing the wisdom of Philippians 2:4, which urges us to *"look not only to your own interests, but also to the interests of others."* Herein lies not just the path to resolution but to mutual growth and understanding.

The Role of Reflection

Reflection is a pivotal exercise in consistently balancing logic with empathy. It involves taking a step back after an interaction to consider not just the argument's facts, but also the emotional currents that flowed throughout the conversation. What fears or hopes were indirectly expressed? How might your words have impacted the other person's feelings? Reflective practices, grounded in faith, care and mindfulness, help us to respond rather than react in future discussions.

Share Your Story

Integrating personal anecdotes can bridge the gap between differing viewpoints. Sharing our stories provides a window into our reasoning and values, making abstract arguments palpable and relatable. Jesus used parables to convey complex spiritual truths; similarly, we can employ our narratives to illustrate points in a relatable and humane way.

Harnessing the Full Spectrum of Persuasion

Ultimately, to persuade is to understand that the full spectrum of human communication includes both logic and emotion. We should aim to match our rhetorical strategies to the multi-dimensional nature of our audience. **Just as a teacher adapts lesson plans to the needs of different students, we must tailor our discourse methods to the varied intellects and emotional makeups of those we engage with.** This sensitivity not only enriches our discussions but empowers us to leave a lasting and positive impact on our collective ability to grapple with the complex issues of our time.

Influence with Intellectual and Emotional Savvy

The ability to navigate debates with both intellectual rigor and a sense of emotional intelligence marks the path toward truly influential communication. James 3:17 guides us by describing wisdom from above as *"first pure, then peaceable, gentle, open to reason, full of mercy and good fruits, impartial and sincere."* **Herein lies an invaluable strategy: to be open to reason — suggestive of logical discourse — while remaining merciful and gentle — an embodiment of empathy.** The business world, too, recognizes the effectiveness of leaders who demonstrate such balanced attributes; their ability to inspire teams and negotiate deals is often grounded in this harmonious blend.

Sharing Knowledge with Empathy

Every interaction offers an opportunity to impart knowledge and wisdom, but the manner in which we do so can either open minds or close hearts. We ought to strive for an approach that honors the other person's perspective, fostering an atmosphere of mutual respect. In my own experience, sharing insights with patience and understanding allows both parties to remain receptive, transforming potential conflicts into collaborative learning experiences.

The Dance of Debate

The art of debate is akin to a dance, requiring partners to move in sync, embracing a rhythm that values both precision and fluidity. **To master this dance, we must be nimble in our logic, presenting clear and concise arguments, while also being attuned to the emotional undercurrents of the discourse.** It's a delicate but powerful dance that can lead to deeper understanding and resolution, much like the professional who must navigate complex negotiations with a deft balance of savvy and sensitivity.

Cultivating the Art of Nuanced Communication

To cultivate the art of nuanced communication, we must be both students and teachers in our engagements. As we learn from others, we also have the responsibility to lead by example, showcasing how respect and understanding can elevate a conversation. We remain humble in our pursuit of knowledge, but firm in our resolve to foster dialogues that bridge divides. By valuing the head and the heart, we do more than converse; we connect, we build, and we thrive.

It is incumbent upon us to care for the truth with the same vigor with which we care for people. By holding intellectual rigor in one hand and sensitivity in the other, we mirror the biblical exhortation to love our neighbors as we love ourselves, respecting both their viewpoints and the emotions that give rise to them. This dual commitment leads to interaction that is not just tolerant but transformative.

Now, take this understanding and weave it into your conversations, your negotiations, and your relationships. Watch as the alchemy of logic and empathy transforms conflicts into connections, creating a symphony of ideas harmonized by the distinct yet complementary notes of intellectual rigor and emotional intelligence.

6

— • —

IDEAS VERSUS IDENTITY

The mid-morning sun cascaded through the stained-glass panes of a modest office where Jacob mused over the worn leather spines of books filled with wisdom of centuries past. The reflected colors danced lightly across his mahogany desk, adorned with a single photo framed in silver — a reminder of a simpler time. It was here, in calming solitude, that Jacob contemplated the nuanced art of debate, a fresh challenge presented by an upcoming public discourse on the intersection of morality and economics.

Sitting back in his chair, he reached for a well-thumbed Bible, its passages a testament to the balance between immutable spiritual truths and the shifting sands of human understanding. As his fingers moved over the verses, he considered how the lessons within could guide him in separating ideas from the very identity of his debate opponent, a fellow scholar renowned for his fiery rhetoric.

Jacob's inner dialogue was a medley of scriptural reflections and strategic musings. "Blessed are the peacemakers," he whispered, contemplating how the Beatitude could anchor his approach, seeking to dissect conflicting economic theories without attacking the person behind them. He envisioned a conversation that, like Solomon's proverbs, was filled with insight and fairness, rather than personal affronts.

An interruption came as a subtle fragrance of incense wafted through the room, a reminder that the church below was preparing for midday mass. Jacob welcomed the scent, considering the ritual it represented as an analogue to the structure of a respectful disagreement — one built on the foundation of tradition and shared beliefs, even when individual interpretations diverged.

His thoughts circled back to his college days when heated debates often turned into ideological battlegrounds, marring friendships and tarnishing respect. He vowed this time would be different; he would embody the grace and patience demonstrated by Christ in His debates with the Pharisees — firm in His convictions yet always dignified and empathetic.

Drawing wisdom from diverse disciplines, from the spiritual to the philosophical, and from economics to politics, Jacob outlined his strategy. He would present with the exacting precision of a seasoned entrepreneur, yet the openness of a teacher eager for mutual enlightenment. His demeanor would be that of a host inviting guests into his home: confident, thoughtful, eager to listen as much as to converse.

As the chime of the church bell marked the hour, Jacob stood with quiet determination. His keen understanding of the significance of his task enveloped him — a sense of duty to demonstrate how one could engage in the most passionate of debates without losing sight of the core Christian principle: love thy neighbor, even when you disagree.

How then, in a world fiercely clinging to polarized views, can the practice of separating ideas from identities become the cornerstone of our engagements, debates, and discussions?

Navigating the Intersection of Ideas and Identity

In an era where the conflation of ideas with identity often leads to polarized impasses, there is a profound need to revisit the principles of respectful disagreement. **Separating ideas from the identities that hold them** is more than an exercise in tolerance; it is an essential foundation for any fruitful discourse. By decoupling the two, we not only honor the sanctity of individual perspective but also pave the way for true understanding and progress.

The heart of the matter lies in the recognition that each person is a mosaic of experiences, beliefs, and emotions — none of which can be wholly defined by a single viewpoint. To effectively engage in a dialogue, especially within the current landscape of diverse thought, **we must focus on the subject of disagreement rather than the personal value of the individuals involved.** Herein lies the path to mastering the art of maintaining mutual respect during debates, a skill critical not only to personal relationships but also to entrepreneurial pursuits, political endeavors and business negotiations.

Drawing upon time-honored spiritual teachings, we are reminded to *"let every person be quick to listen, slow to speak, slow to anger"* (James 1:19). This scriptural wisdom encapsulates the spirit required for separating ideas from identity. Patience and attentiveness become the bedrock upon which disagreements can transform into meaningful exchanges rather than breeding grounds for conflict.

Engaging with contrasting viewpoints while avoiding identity-based conflicts demands a delicate balance. This balance often requires an entrepreneurial resilience analogous to navigating market competition — it entails striving for success amidst differing strategies without undermining the integrity or value of the competitors. Applying this to our discussions means embracing diversity of thought as a welcome challenge rather than a threat to one's personal identity.

The Craft of Civil Discourse

The strategic importance of focus on the subject of disagreement cannot be overstated. Like any thought leader or visionary, **the goal is not to diminish one's opponent but to elevate the conversation. This elevates both parties, transforming adversaries into collaborators. By dissecting issues rather than dissecting characters**, we cultivate a terrain where innovative ideas can germinate alongside mutual respect.

Moreover, leaders across various fields — from theology to politics, economics to social activism — demonstrate that acknowledging the diversity of human identity enriches the discourse. By appreciating the multifaceted nature of individuals, we move closer to solutions that are encompassing and sustainable. A negotiation, after all, thrives on the syntheses of differing viewpoints, not on their annihilation.

Personal anecdotes abound which affirm this approach: CEOs resolving company direction stalemates, community leaders bridging cultural divides, individuals surpassing personal impasses — all examples where separation of idea from identity has made cooperation possible. These are not mere instances of compromise but of a higher synthesis where all involved emerge with enhanced understanding and respect.

Masterful Respect Amidst Adversity

To navigate these treacherous waters, entrepreneurs and business leaders alike must develop the acumen to detach ideas from the personal domains they are often entangled with. **It is a strategy that eschews shortsighted gains for long-term relational stability and growth**. By reframing disagreement as an integral, even healthy, part of the human experience, we foster an environment where the friction of dissent sparks innovation rather than ignites conflicts.

Let us, therefore, endeavor to see beyond the veil of our convictions to the space where dialogue lives. Let it be steeped in mutual respect, insulated from the tempests of identity politics. This is the crucible in which ideas are tested, refined, and where the potential for harmony in dissent is realized. As we embrace this challenge with a steady hand and an open heart, we not only become more effective communicators and leaders but also custodians of a world more empathetic and united in its diversity.

In essence, the mastery of this principle not only shapes our debates but also reflects our intrinsic humanity — our capacity for empathy, understanding, and growth. It is through this lens that we can see disagreement not as an impasse but as the very instrument by which we can forge stronger, more innovative paths forward, together.

When engaging in debate, it's essential to recognize the distinction between a person's thoughts and his or her core self. This practice transforms contentious interactions into opportunities for growth and understanding. **Ideas are mutable**, the fruit borne from one's experiences and knowledge, perpetually ripe for change. **An individual's identity, however, is the bedrock of his or her existence —** intrinsic and fundamentally consistent. Linking the two is like tying a boat to a freely drifting buoy—it may follow for a while but will ultimately falter when the seas of discourse become turbulent.

Addressing someone's point of view as a mere extension of their identity can inadvertently dismiss the dynamic nature both of ideas and of the human spirit. Spiritual teachings guide us to love one another, to entreat each other with compassion, which becomes challenging when disagreements are misconstrued as personal attacks. Scriptures teach that we are more alike than different in our cores, so when we separate someone's ideas from who they are at heart, we pay homage to the spiritual principle of unity.

In the business realm, this separation facilitates innovation and collaboration. The most visionary entrepreneurs understand that effective critique hones ideas to their finest point. When a proposal is debated, it is not a referendum on the proposer but an investment in refining a concept for the benefit of the project. This approach not only preserves professional relationships but also propels them forward; **colleagues feel more comfortable being candid knowing that their worth is not on trial.**

From an entrepreneurial perspective, perseverance is key — a trait best nurtured in environments that encourage free exchange of thoughts without the fear of personal reproach. **Each idea should be considered a building block that may or may not fit at the time, rather than a scathing criticism of a person's value or character.** By separating ideas from identity, we fashion a scaffold from which everyone can ascend together in pursuit of excellence.

Theology, politics, and economics all present fields where the conflation of ideas with identity can lead to unnecessary strife. Historical schisms within religious communities, polarized political environments, and market crashes influenced by herd mentality exemplify the dangers of such entanglement. On the contrary, approaching these fields with the understanding that our shared humanity supersedes our differing opinions paves the way for enlightened cooperation and progress.

Reflecting upon personal experiences, it's not hard to recall situations where our own ideas were evolving, in flux. To have been judged based on those ideas alone would discount the depths of our character, our potential for change. In sharing these stories, we uncover a common ground, a recognition that respect is owed to the nuanced tapestry of identity that extends beyond the confines of transient thoughts and beliefs.

Fostering a Culture of Respectful Discourse

Maintaining this distinction becomes a dance of wisdom, a deliberate step in fostering tolerant societies and productive work environments. When we achieve a balance, treating ideas as separate from the soul, **we lay the groundwork for a culture that engages with topics rigorously, yet never loses sight of the inherent dignity of its participants. It's about cultivating a setting where minds can change without losing face, where progress is measured not in victories over others, but in the collective advancement of understanding.**

The next step in mastering this artful distinction is to zoom in on the subject of disagreement itself, stripping away the personal and focusing on the shared goal of finding truth or solving a problem. Here, we delve into the crucial tactics for navigating the substance of a debate without allowing it to become mired in questions of personal value.

The Value of Ideological Neutrality

While remaining neutral in disputes might sound counterproductive, there's profound strength in it. We ought to approach disagreements with an understanding that **ideas are not the sum total of a person's value. A commitment to this principle is reflected in the ancient wisdom of "hate the sin, love the sinner", which can be pragmatically translated into modern discourse as critiquing the idea, not the person**. This enables us to foster an environment where critique is seen not as an attack, but as a catalyst for growth and learning. In a business context, it means may the best idea win, regardless of who voices it, promoting a culture of merit and innovation.

The Art of Dispassionate Deliberation

Encouraging dispassionate deliberation does not mean that we must strip away passion for our causes; rather, it necessitates channeling our fervor into a structured, reasoned argument. It is within our engagements that **we demonstrate restraint by focusing on the facts rather than allowing personal feelings to drive the conversation**. This is a skill honed by successful negotiators, debaters, and mediators. By operationalizing this within our own debates, we not only become more effective communicators but also protect the integrity and respect due to all participants.

The Constructive Use of Disagreement

Disagreement, when wielded appropriately, can be a tool for sharpening our understanding and refining our propositions. Theologians debate interpretations, economists argue over policy impacts, and entrepreneurs challenge each other's business strategies — all with the aim of reaching a higher truth or more effective solution. By embracing this approach, we stand to gain deeper insights and more resilient conclusions, creating space for innovation and progress.

Avoiding Identity-Based Conflict

To avoid sliding into identity-based conflict, we must be the stewards of our own discourse, defusing tensions by redirecting conversations to the topics at hand. This is not just about being polite; it is about being strategic, **maintaining the dialogue's focus, and getting to the heart of the matter. When debates become personal, they often become unproductive.** Instead, let us exemplify respect for divergent views and anchor our interactions in the spirit of constructive, idea-based dialogue.

The Harmony Framework

In the bustling marketplace of ideas, our goal is to navigate through disagreements with poise and respect. The Harmony Framework provides a blueprint to achieve this end, acting as a compass to guide us through the tumultuous waves of debate without losing sight of our shared humanity or mutual respect. Let's delve into each crucial step of this framework to enhance our analytical skills and foster dialogues marked by understanding and empathy.

Identify the Main Claim

At the heart of every debate lies a central claim, a thesis that anchors all subsequent reasoning. Identifying this main claim is akin to finding the keystone in an arch; remove it, and the entire structure falters. By concentrating on this pivotal point, we move closer to grasping the essence of the argument, which allows us to engage with the content of the discussion rather than the character of the individual.

Evaluate Supporting Evidence

Once we've pinpointed the core argument, the next step is to scrutinize the supporting evidence. Examining evidence akin to analyzing the bricks that build the foundation of a claim. We assess their durability, their relevance, and whether they're genuinely supportive or merely decorative. High-quality, reliable evidence strengthens an argument, just as strong bricks support a robust structure.

Assess Logical Reasoning

The architecture of an argument is held together by the mortar of logic. When assessing the logical reasoning, we inspect the cohesiveness of the argument. Are there any cracks in the logic, any fallacies that might cause the argument to crumble under scrutiny? Just as a building must be evaluated for its structural integrity, so too must an argument for its logical coherence.

Consider Counterarguments

The final cornerstone of The Harmony Framework involves engaging with counterarguments. This endeavor is not merely a defense against potential critiques but an active search for alternative viewpoints that challenge the main claim. Like testing a structure against the elements, engaging with opposing perspectives ensures that the argument can withstand the sometimes harsh winds of criticism while also allowing for a richer, more dynamic understanding of the subject.

Practical Implications of The Harmony Framework

The Harmony Framework isn't merely theoretical; it's a practical toolkit. In a world where the zeal for one's viewpoints can often lead to contentious disputes, it provides a method to navigate conflict with dignity and intelligence. It encourages the seeker of truth to be both a diligent critic and a humble student, maintaining a balance between assertiveness and openness. For the entrepreneur, it is a way to dissect and engage with diverse business strategies critically. For the spiritual, it's a guided approach that resonates with a quest for deeper understanding.

Future Development and Application

As with any analytical tool, The Harmony Framework is dynamic and adaptable. It is pertinent in discussions ranging from theology and philosophy to the intricacies of politics and economics. By providing a structure that is both rigorous and respectful, this framework has the potential to transform the discourse, paving the way for debates that enrich and enlighten rather than demean and divide.

Let this framework be a beacon on your path to discernment, a testament to the belief that even in a world brimming with discord, harmony is not only possible but essential. With thoughtful application, The Harmony Framework empowers us to engage in respectful disagreement, ensuring that our discourse is characterized by civility, curiosity, and a shared pursuit of truth in the complexity of our times.

A Harmonious Path Forward

By embracing diversity of thought, we can mold our disagreements into building blocks for a stronger society. This challenge is not for the faint of heart or for the lazy — it calls for courage, patience, and a commitment to personal growth. Let us then, with the humble confidence of the wise, continue to transform our conflicts into connections, aiming to not only debate effectively but also to enhance the fabric of our shared humanity.

7

THE ART OF ACTIVE LISTENING

I n the golden warmth of a late afternoon, the streets of a bustling city exuded the rhythm of a thousand stories, each soul a character in the grand tapestry of life. John, an entrepreneur with a heart kindled by faith, moved through the crowd, his mind swirling with conversation from an earlier meeting. Like a chess player deliberating a critical move, he pondered each word exchanged, seeking to embody the virtues his spiritual practice extolled. The crux of the discussion: a potential partnership that demanded not just keen business acumen but moral discernment.

Every step he took through the market district, the sights and sounds played into the symphony of his thoughts. Fruit vendors called out the ripeness of their wares, horns blared from impatient drivers, and friends greeted each other with laughter that cut through the din. These were the melodies of human endeavor, echoing the work he too was embroiled in — endeavors not merely for profit but for purpose. John's mind was a ground fertile for the seeds of inspiration, his beliefs the water that nurtured them into actions that reached beyond self-interest.

His hand brushed along the railings as he walked, the cool metal a tiny oasis in the heat. A moment of introspection was bathed in the crisp scent of autumn air, a prelude to the setting sun. He thought about the verses of scripture he read that morning, the ones urging integrity and stewardship, which aligned so closely with his entrepreneurial journey. An orphanage nearby, a structure of modest means but immeasurable love, reminded him keenly of why he had chosen this path.

The people he passed mirrored reflections of his own resolve. There was the young artist, her eyes aglow with the passion of creation, canvases under her arm. And the old watchmaker, whose steady hands spoke of years crafting time, his shop a capsule of a slowly vanishing era. John saw in them the essence of what his spiritual teachings impressed upon him: that each was called to contribute uniquely, to thread their gifts into the weave of humanity.

At a corner café, a group of vibrant thinkers debated with fierce intensity, their words a dance of ideas. Drawn by the allure of their exchange, he listened — not merely to respond but to understand. The practice of active listening, a skill he refined with every interaction, now allowed him to grasp the fabric of their thoughts, to empathize with the emotions woven into their reasoning. Perhaps, he contemplated, it was such respectful discourse that could illuminate the path for his business venture.

As the sun dipped below the high-rises, casting amber streams across the pavement, John's mind alighted on a plan solidified by prayer, persistence, and the pursuit of purpose. Yet, with the prospect of tomorrow's decision looming, a question lingered, fragrant as the twilight air itself: How might the guidance of revered spiritual principles steer the forthcoming choices on his venture, and what new chapters would those choices inscribe in the narrative of his life's work?

Listen to Connect, Not to Counter

Active listening is often hailed as the unsung hero of effective communication and the cornerstone of understanding. **Yet in a world that's rapidly polarizing, its power is frequently overlooked. This is particularly true in the midst of debate, where the knee-jerk reaction is to form a rebuttal rather than to comprehend the essence of another's words.** Here within these pages lies a clarion call to embrace active listening as an indispensable tool in the arsenal of anyone who seeks not just to persuade, but also to foster genuine connections in discussions that matter.

The sacred texts across various faiths extol the virtue of listening. Proverbs 18:13 teaches, *"To answer before listening — that is folly and shame."* This ancient wisdom holds modern relevance; it underpins the belief that truly listening is an act of respect and humility. In an age where discord is rife, adopting this scriptural guidance paves the way for more meaningful discourse. By practicing active listening, we show reverence for our conversational counterparts, allowing for a more empathetic and informed response to the viewpoints they present.

In the crucible of debate, we are called to do more than merely hear; we are called to listen with intent. The ability to dissect and digest opposing ideas is what transforms a conversation from a series of monologues into a dynamic dialectic. To foster this transformation is to venture onto the path of wisdom. Such a path requires patience and commitment, yes, yet it also promises the reward of deepening our understanding of the complex mosaic that is human thought.

Business leaders and entrepreneurs can attest that mastering the art of active listening is not merely an esoteric exercise; it's a practical strategy that drives success. When we listen actively, we are gathering the threads of another's reasoning, weaving it into our own fabric of understanding, and hence responding with acumen and precision. This ability is especially crucial when tackling the harder grains of truth that often emerge in negotiations or team collaborations.

Amidst the teachings of Scripture, we're reminded to *"let every person be quick to hear, slow to speak, slow to anger; for the anger of man does not produce the righteousness of God"* (James 1:19-20). This directive serves as a touchstone for those wishing to engage in thoughtful debate. It encourages us to pause, to internalize and reflect upon the words of others before formulating our response. In the context of discourse, this means that active listening is an act of grace, one that quells the fires of conflict and illuminates the path to resolution.

Embarking on this journey, it is essential to recognize that active listening is not an inherent talent; it is a skill cultivated through conscious practice and dedication. It's a discipline that beckons each of us to forge ahead with intention, laying the groundwork for robust and meaningful dialogue that transcends mere words and reaches the heart of mutual understanding.

Let us therefore step forward with the affirmation that by honing our listening, we do more than enhance our conversational capabilities; we engage in an act of transformation, both of self and society. And so, as you progress through the wisdom contained herein, be prepared to unlock the latent power within, fostering harmony where once there was dissent.

Active listening isn't just a good habit; it's an indispensable ally in the delicate dance of debate. When we converse about the intricacies of any subject, from the deeply personal to the abstractly theoretical, there lies the potential for transformative dialogue or combustible discord. The difference often hinges on our ability to genuinely listen. The Bible tells us, *"Everyone should be quick to listen, slow to speak and slow to become angry, for human anger does not produce the righteousness that God desires"* (James 1:19-20). This ancient wisdom holds a contemporary truth — **quieting our own voice to magnify another's can grant us insights previously clouded by our biases and preconceptions.**

To truly debate the merits of an idea, we must move beyond the superficial exchange. **It involves submerging yourself in the speaker's words, sympathizing with their perspective, and seeking to understand their emotional undercurrents.** Leaders in business, politics, education and ministry who master this skill are not only more persuasive but also more perceivable as empathetic and trustworthy. Think of active listening as the scaffolding upon which robust discussions are constructed — without it, any attempt at meaningful discourse is liable to crumble.

At the heart of active listening is the commitment to shifting from a focus on responding to a dedication to comprehending more fully what someone else said. In the throes of a debate, it's easy to be caught up in one's thoughts or preparing a retort while the other person is speaking. However, this approach will almost certainly detract from the richness of what's being shared. **To adopt active listening is to enter a conversation with a mindset akin to an investigator — seeking clarity, asking probing questions, and displaying genuine curiosity about the layers of thought that shape the other's viewpoint.**

Active listening extends to recognizing and validating emotions, not just facts. In a corporate setting where logic often prevails, acknowledging the emotive drivers behind a colleague's rationale can diffuse tension and open avenues for more nuanced understanding. **When individuals feel heard at a core level, they are more open to finding common ground and more willing to consider alternative perspectives.** The fulfillment of this principle can be found in the words of the proverb: *"As iron sharpens iron, so one person sharpens another"* (Proverbs 27:17). In this exchange of ideas, there is a mutual strengthening — a dual honing of intellect — that requires the whetstone of active listening.

The rudiments of active listening lie not only in silencing our speech but in attuning all our senses to the person before us. **Our body language, eye contact, and even moments of silence communicate a profound respect for what the speaker has to say.** When we actively listen, we are not passive absorbers but dynamic enactors of a holistic communication process. The political leader who harnesses this art demonstrates a caliber of professionalism and human respect that elevates his or her interactions to a higher standard.

Yet active listening is not a skill that blossoms overnight. Like any worthy endeavor, it necessitates intentional practice and continuous refinement. **Begin by resolving to focus on the speaker more ardently in your next conversation, resisting distractions, interruptions, and the allure of quick conclusions.** As you develop the discipline of listening to understand, rather than to reply, you slowly encounter the rich tapestry of human experience that previously lay just beyond your notice.

Remember, we live in a symphony of voices, each contributing a unique melody to the collective narrative. To participate fully in this orchestral life, we must learn not only when to raise our voice but — perhaps more importantly — **when to listen so we may harmonize with others**. In the context of debate, active listening enables us to grasp the conductor's baton with grace, guiding the discourse towards a masterpiece of collaborative thought rather than a discordant clamor.

Understanding Opposing Viewpoints

In the art of debate, **it's crucial to recognize that the foundation of a meaningful exchange lies in our ability to comprehend differing perspectives**. In practice, this goes beyond just passive hearing. It entails a conscious effort to empathize with the other party's viewpoint. Ancient wisdom teaches that the highest form of knowledge is to know and understand others. By rooting our efforts in such principles, we cultivate a spirit of respectful engagement, peering through the lens of another's experience with an intent to learn rather than to confront. This deepened understanding equips us to form responses that are not only well-informed but also imbued with empathy.

Fostering Empathy in Responses

Empathy, as spiritual texts often elucidate, **is not merely feeling alongside others but bearing the weight of their thoughts and emotions as if they were our own**. When we respond in debate, our words should reflect that we have grappled with the other person's ideas, acknowledging the validity in their concerns. Embodying this quality in our discourse, we make space for a collective journey towards truth. A response that illustrates empathy doesn't mirror agreement but indicates a profound respect for the dignity of the other individual's perspective.

Respectful Engagement

Demonstrating respect in dialogue is a cornerstone of progress. **When we regard others' thoughts as worthy of consideration, we man-**

ifest an underlying respect that is essential for constructive interaction. It may help to consider the biblical adage, popularly known
as the Golden Rule, *"Do unto others as you would have them do unto
you."* Applied to debate, this principle advocates for a discourse
that honors the other as an equal contributor to the exchange.
This does not mean shying away from disagreement but engaging in a
way that upholds the mutual respect fundamental for breakthroughs
in understanding.

Laying the Groundwork for Dialogue

It is our duty to set a foundation for robust dialogue. In doing so,
we must avoid the pitfalls of superficial agreement and aim for
a space where ideas can be tested and refined. Reminiscent of
the marketplace of ideas, this space allows for the free exchange and
competition of thoughts. It is where we tune out the noise of egos and
tune in to the substance and merits of the conversation. Our approach
in laying this groundwork should mirror the patience of a seasoned
farmer tending to the soil, understanding that the fruits of such labor
may not be immediate but the eventual yield will be enriched by our
attentiveness.

Crafting Responses

In fashioning responses, let us be as an architect, constructing our
retort with careful choice of words and structure. Our statements
should reflect a clarity of thought and intention, akin to laying bricks
with mortar that is both strong and pliable. We are called to reinforce
our responses with substance while maintaining the flexibility to adapt
and evolve our perspective. This skill, much like a bridge, supports

constructive exchanges and connects disparate viewpoints with understanding and grace.

Mastery Through Perseverance

In mastering the skills required for active listening and empathetic response, it is imperative to persevere. In the context of debate, this translates to embracing each opportunity for dialogue as a step closer towards proficiency. With each attempt, we brush up against our imperfections but also polish our talents, cultivating a versatility in thought and expression that is priceless in the pursuit of collective enlightenment.

Personal Anecdotes as a Bridge to Empathy

Recall a time when you felt truly heard. The sense of validation and respect you likely experienced in that moment is what you aim to offer in discussions with others. By drawing upon your experiences of being respectfully listened to, you can better understand the importance of reciprocating that gift of attention. Sharing personal anecdotes related to active listening can serve as powerful examples, highlighting the transformative power of a respectful dialogue on both a personal and business level.

The Tapestry of Varied Perspectives

In the vast tapestry of human interaction, each thread of perspective adds strength and color to the whole. By integrating insights from theology to politics, from economics to personal relationships, we mirror the diversity of experiences that inform our viewpoints. Treating these varied perspectives with respect means acknowledging their validity, even when we disagree. This approach not only demonstrates our expertise and openness to learning but also enriches the discourse, allowing for a more comprehensive understanding of the issues at hand.

The Dance of Dialogical Exchange

Engaging in dialogue is akin to a dance where each partner is attentive to the other's moves and rhythm. As you listen actively, allow the conversation to flow naturally, with turns taken and responses offered in a rhythm that respects both parties' need to express themselves. This form of exchange is the bedrock of robust and meaningful dialogue. It upholds the conviction that every voice holds value, and through this mutual recognition, the potential for enlightenment and consensus is amplified.

The Power of Persuasive Patience

In a world where immediacy often trumps reflection, active listening is an act of persuasive patience. **It is the strength to hold space for another's words as if they were your own, the capacity to digest and respond with grace. Exercise this patience and you'll find it becomes a compelling force, one that persuades others not through the volume or immediacy of your words, but through the evidence of your genuine engagement with theirs.** By embodying the principles of thoughtful listening and respectful discourse, you become a catalyst for change, fostering more connection in a more polarized world.

Honing Your Listening Craft

Listening is not a static skill but a craft to be honed continually. Diverse viewpoints challenge us to refine our ability to listen and respond respectfully. Encourage yourself to practice, to persevere, and to become proficient in the art of active listening. The rewards are manifold — strengthened relationships, enhanced understanding, and discussions brimming with constructive, creative potential. The mastery of this craft stands to benefit not only your personal and business interactions but to ripple outward, contributing to a more harmonious society.

The Imperative of Active Listening

Active listening is not merely a passive act; it is the cornerstone of engaging in meaningful debate and understanding. Active listening embodies the respect and consideration we must show each other, allowing diverse thoughts to coalesce into fruitful discussions and potential collaborations.

Fostering Empathy through Understanding

The ability to interpret and internalize perspectives that differ from our own is a skill that requires patience and practice. Proverbs 18:2 warns against folly in the lack of understanding; thus, we must diligently cultivate the aptitude to listen with an intent to comprehend rather than to merely reply. By developing empathetic responses, our retorts become reflective of a deeper awareness, one that acknowledges the values and experiences behind an opposing view.

This practice not only enriches our perspectives but, more importantly, dignifies the individual presenting them.

Stepping Stones to Eloquent Exchange

Persuasion rests upon the clarity of our speech and the cogence of our arguments. Yet it is the silent moments of attentive listening that give weight to our words. Entrepreneurs and business leaders know that successful negotiations hinge on understanding the other party's position — it is the blueprint for any strategic interaction. Similarly, in the art of debate, we must listen actively, fully engage with the content presented to us, and respond with precision and thoughtfulness.

A Warm Invitation to Action

Let us then embrace active listening not as a mere technique, but as a way of being that reflects our deepest values and convictions. **The ability to truly hear out a counterpart conveys a warmth that can turn opponents into allies and dissension into harmony**. I encourage you to embark on this journey with a steadfast heart and an open mind. Let your actions speak to the reverence you have for the act of listening, and let your growth in this art be a testament to your commitment to fostering genuine connections in all aspects of your life.

Embrace today as an opportunity to sharpen your active listening skills, fortify your empathetic responses, and demonstrate irrefutable respect in every conversation. Embark on this path not only for the betterment of debate but as a building block for enduring relationships and successful business endeavors. Remember, the profound act of listening is an offering of peace in a world that clamors for attention

— be the listener who stands out, and in doing so, create a legacy of thought leadership and impactful dialogue.

8

GOOD SPORTSMANSHIP IN DISCOURSE

In the dim warmth of a family-owned bookstore, nestled in the heart of the bustling city, Michael stood absorbed in the thoughts that circled like the sparrow outside – agile and uncatchable. His gaze, however, rested not on the pages before him but through the window, where life danced to the rhythm of unseen music. The musky scent of old books blended seamlessly with the coffee aroma wafting from the next street, crafting an atmosphere most conducive to pensive reflection.

The issue at hand, that which ruffled his spirits more than it should, was a simple debate from yesterday's gathering. Like a persistent wind that refused to settle, the unresolved exchange about economic policies beckoned him with invisible fingers. Untying those knots was not just a mental exercise but an ethical conundrum, and his friends' differing perspectives echoed like whispers from a forgotten dream. Change in dialogue was not just inevitable; it was necessary, he recalled, a mantra from one of the ancient texts he so reverently poured over.

A bell jingled as a patron departed, pulling Michael back from his reverie. Yet the interruption was brief; he soon dove inward once more, drawing upon past endeavors where perseverance turned barren fields of debate into lush gardens of consensus. Disagreement was not meant to be a personal slight but the friction necessary to ignite the spark of progress and understanding.

Clutching at these thoughts, he looked around at the shelves that cradled wisdom of ages, reminded of his journey. Once a zealous entrepreneur who clashed with every opposing view, now he sought the tranquil middle ground where ideas could dance without trampling each other's feet. A spirited debate was, to his maturing mind, akin to the intricate steps of a tango – passionate yet respectful, fervent but always elegant.

A child's laughter punctured his contemplation, bringing him a smile. It was a simple reminder that life, with its myriad voices, was learning incarnate. Each dialogue, each collision of viewpoints, was a stepping stone laid on the path to growth. Clasping his book close, as if to draw strength from its bound wisdom, Michael entertained the thought of invigorating discussions yet to come, painting his journey with broad strokes drawn from diverse fields.

As the sun set, casting deep orange hues into the room, Michael pondered the delicate balance of staying grounded in his beliefs yet open to the ever changing tides of discourse. Could one's steadfastness be a vessel, not an anchor, in the fluid seas of intellectual exchange?

The Art of Agreeing to Disagree

The fabric of society is woven from strands of numerous perspectives, each varying in background, experience, and insight. In a landscape often marred by division, finding a common thread of respect and understanding in the tapestry of human interaction is not just idealistic — it's essential for progress. **Good sportsmanship in dialogue is the golden rule that can often be overlooked in the heat of a debate**

yet is the very principle that can lead us from discord to a richer, more nuanced understanding of one another. Clearly, good sportsmanship should not be reserved to high school teams shaking hands after an athletic game or to Pop Warner football for younger children. Good sportsmanship definitely has a place in our "adulting" phase, especially in a world that has many sore losers who raise anarchy if they do not get their way in winning by any means necessary, even if the means are questionable or even unethical. In the domain of exchange — where ideas compete ideally in a free marketplace, and beliefs are respectfully challenged — it's crucial to recall that **the true victory lies not in dominance, but in the collective leap towards greater awareness, empathy and resolution together**.

The process of embracing diversity of thought requires a dual commitment — to steadfastly present one's viewpoint, and simultaneously to hold space for opposition with grace and flexibility. It begins by accepting that changing viewpoints and unresolved debates are not the markings of failure but rather the hallmarks of a dynamic and healthy conversation. Acknowledging the evolving nature of discourse serves as a reminder that the human mind is in a constant state of flux, capable of growth and adaptation. It's a sign that we are engaged, active participants in the collective endeavor of building knowledge and understanding.

To navigate through conversations with this ethos, **one must cultivate an attitude untethered from the personal ego. Our self-worth and worthiness of love and respect from others are not contingent upon others agreeing with us. Disagreements should not be seen as personal slights, but rather as opportunities for self-reflection and communal learning**. This perceptual shift requires the deliberate practice of emotional intelligence and the willingness to separate one's self-worth from one's ideas. **By fostering** this detachment, we create room for our ideas to be dissected and discussed without fear of vulnerability or offense — a true test of our commitment to dialogue.

Encouraging a growth mindset is key. Each discussion, whether it propagates agreement or breeds debate, is a vessel for learning. **Such a mindset celebrates the journey of intellectual exploration, where the winning outcome — while often desired — is not the sole prize**. By prioritizing comprehension over victory, **we align ourselves more closely with truth-seeking than ego-affirming**. The pursuit of collective understanding, the sharpening of one's reasoning, the openness in the environment to debate again on another issue with a respectful partner, and the expansion of our worldviews are treasures in themselves, culminating in a spirit of inquiry that propels societies forward.

Crafting Good Sportsmanship in Debates: A Guide

1. **Define the purpose and goals**: This initial step provides direction, ensuring everyone involved understands the target they are collectively aiming for. Whether the goal is to generate solutions, unpack complex issues, or simply to understand differing perspectives, clarity of intention sets the stage for meaningful exchange.

2. **Establish discussion guidelines**: Herein lies the framework within which respectful and fruitful conversations can flourish. Active listening, mutual respect, no name-calling, and evidence-based argumentation become the normative pillars upholding the sanctity of civil discourse, creating a sanctuary where ideas can be safely exchanged and examined.

3. **Set a structured agenda**: Like a map guiding explorers, a structured agenda delineates the path of the conversation, ensuring that the topics are addressed in a focused and orderly fashion. Giving participants a glimpse of the discussion's landscape beforehand empowers them to contribute effectively and with confidence.

4. **Encourage equal participation**: A democratic approach to discussion invites input from all sides, not just the two most popular and diametrically opposed viewpoints, raising the value of the deliberation. This egalitarian spirit fosters harmony and nurtures the seeds of collective intelligence, nourishing the ground for an enriched understanding to bloom regarding the issue at hand.

5. **Foster open-mindedness**: A mind open to new perspectives is where the magic of transformation begins. Here, the encouragement to pause judgment and to embrace novelty is pivotal, harking back to the age-old wisdom that in the multitude of counselors, there is victory.

6. **Manage conflicts effectively**: Conflicts, when navigated with poise and respect, can be the very incidences that lead to breakthroughs and further exploration. As facilitators, we must ensure that respect underpins every argument and that resolution is sought with the intent of agreement, rather than triumph.

7. **Summarize key points and outcomes**: To remember and to clarify — that is the aim of summarizing. Through it, partners can respectfully shake hands after the discus-

sion, recognizing both its convergences and divergences, and weaving together the collective output and potential solutions of the conversation, as well as next steps following the debate.

As we look ahead in this chapter, let us remember that our discourse is, at its core, a reflection of our shared humanity. It is a manifestation of our desire to understand and to be understood — a pursuit that, while it may not always lead to agreement, can always lead to a deeper connection with the worlds within and around us. Through these shared dialogues, we weave a world enriched by diversity, grounded in respect, and elevated by the shared commitment to learn and grow together.

Embracing the Dynamic Nature of Perspectives

One of the most profound lessons drawn from the rich repository of spiritual wisdom is the understanding that change is integral to life. In the context of conversations and debate, this means accepting that viewpoints are inherently dynamic, not static. Just as seasons transition and rivers flow, human perspectives are designed to evolve. It's crucial to approach dialogue with the openness to this natural ebb and flow, rather than with rigid expectations of immediate consensus. Holding onto the belief that opinions are immovable objects can lead to frustration and unnecessary confrontation during exchanges.

Recognize that disagreements are part and parcel of discourse, not anomalies to be avoided. Reframing unresolved debates as opportunities for further reflection and education acknowledges that the journey towards truth is iterative and that sometimes the best resolution is an acknowledgment of

our differences, coupled with the commitment to continue the dialogue.

The business world often rewards decisiveness and clarity, yet it also values visionary thinkers who can adapt to change. In conversations, particularly those revolving around ideas and strategies, **flexibility can be a greater asset than unwavering firmness. Acknowledging the potential fluidity of opinions may lead to more innovative solutions and stronger collaborative efforts.**

Take for instance a business negotiation where both parties come to the table with distinct objectives. The early discussions likely involve presenting and defending one's initial standpoint. However, **a truly fruitful business discussion evolves when each party proactively shares where they are flexible and where they are non-negotiable, begins to adapt over the course of respectfully listening to one another, integrates new information from the other viewpoint, and potentially alters his or her position from the start of their discussion that could lead to a stronger compromise and solution that fits for both parties involved.** This process of negotiation is not a sign of weakness but rather a display of strategic adaptability.

Maintaining a respectful dialogue is tantamount to fostering an environment of continuous learning. As an entrepreneur or working professional, you are often taught to bring solutions, to be the one with the answers. However, adapting to changing viewpoints within discourse is much like navigating a complex marketplace; **it requires not only confidence in your current knowledge but also a willingness to pivot when new opportunities, facts or challenges emerge.** Just as market conditions change and strategies must follow suit, discussions can lead to new understandings that warrant a shift in perspective.

It is equally important to model this behavior for others, demonstrating that adapting viewpoints is an acceptable and celebrated part of a healthy dialogue. When leaders and peers exemplify this openness, it cultivates a culture where ideas can be challenged and reformed without fear of reprisal or humiliation. Embodying this principle can positively influence team dynamics, client relationships, and personal growth. It positions one as a thought leader who is secure enough to evolve when faced with compelling arguments or new evidence.

Remember, enduring insights often emerge from the alliance of disparate ideas. To be steadfast in the pursuit of understanding is to appreciate the symphony of voices, each contributing unique notes to the greater whole. Rather than viewing resolution as the only measure of a successful discourse, seek to value the rich texture that varied opinions bring to our interactions.

The Art of Detachment

Detachment is a concept well-versed in theology, often cited as a pathway to spiritual peace. Similarly, **in conversations, detaching oneself from *the need to be right* allows for a more contemplative and less confrontational exchange.** When we enter discussions with the understanding that our perspectives are not the sum total of our identity, disagreements transform from personal threats to exploratory dialogues. Learning to view discourse as a collective journey rather than a battle to be won enriches not only our own intellect but also our collective wisdom.

Growth Through Diversity of Thought

In the Bible, we are reminded to *"speak the truth in love"* (Ephesians 4:15), implying a balance of honesty and compassion. Similarly, when engaging in discourse, we should advocate for our own viewpoints with vigor while also cherishing the diversity that differing opinions bring to our collective table. It is in the richness of varied perspectives where we often find the seeds of growth and innovation. **The ability to discuss these diverse viewpoints without feeling insecure in oneself or personally attacked is a hallmark of a mature and emotionally intelligent individual** — traits revered in spiritual, political, academic, family and business domains.

Fostering a Culture of Openness

To foster a culture of openness, one must cultivate the spirit of a learner, always willing to be taught by others. We can all learn something from somebody. In the world of academia, the highest regard is often given to those who can maintain the curiosity of a student. A spirit of inquisitiveness keeps the doors of personal and professional development forever open. Approaching discourse with a question rather than a statement can shift the dynamics from one of contention to one of shared exploration. It is this shared journey of discovery that can bring us closer together, irrespective of the differences in our initial stances.

The Value of Patience in Dialogue

Patience is regarded as a virtue across many spiritual traditions and is essential for maintaining decorum in any discussion. The most effective negotiators and mediators understand that wise counsel and the best solutions often emerge from tolerant and measured interaction. Racing to conclusions or pushing for immediate agreement can be counterproductive; instead, giving the dialogue time to unfold naturally honors the process of collective understanding. With patience, we can navigate discussions, ensuring that everyone feels heard and valued.

The Art of Civil Conversation

In the practice of good sportsmanship in discourse, there is a fine line between assertively stating one's case and becoming intransigently wedded to one's views. The art of civil conversation mirrors the foundational principles found in countless spiritual texts: to act with love, to respect our neighbor's voice, and to seek understanding as we explore potential solutions together. This is wisdom that transcends any single dialogue — it is a life philosophy that, when applied, enhances the way we connect with others and, ultimately, the way we view the world and the potential that our world can be. Embodying these principles in our discussions assures that we remain open to growth and learning, whatever the outcome of the discourse may be.

The Classroom of Everyday Conversations

Consider for a moment that our conversations are akin to a dynamic classroom where the syllabus is the shared knowledge and experiences of the participants. The role of student and teacher constantly interchange as we absorb and impart wisdom. This is a humbling reframing of dialogues, where every person you encounter might teach you something valuable, provided you are willing to listen. In the business realm, adopting such a stance can lead to innovative ideas and strategies, often emerging from the most unanticipated sources. Theologians, too, recognize that wisdom may come from the mouths of young people, and in our dialogues, this translates to keeping our minds poised for enrichment, regardless of its origin.

Channels of Continuous Improvement

In the pursuit of personal and professional mastery, continuous improvement is a core principle. **Every dialogue should be seen as an opportunity to refine your argumentation skills, your listening ability, and your capacity to empathize with differing viewpoints**. The capacity to adapt and learn from each interaction is a hallmark of not only intellectual agility but also of emotional intelligence — a quality highly valued in leadership within entrepreneurial, political, business, and theological endeavors. As *"iron sharpens iron"* in Proverbs 27:17, the interactions where our ideas are challenged invariably serve to sharpen our minds and either strengthen our convictions or reshape them for the better.

Live to Debate Another Day

Civil discourse can be likened to an *infinite game*, once popularized by author Simon Sinek, **where the goal isn't to win but to keep playing the game** — to perpetuate the exchange of ideas and the broadening of perspectives. In such a game, success is measured not by the dominance of an idea, but by the fluidity and adaptivity of your thought processes. This is not to suggest an aimless conversation but one that is purposeful in its openness — the richness of a dialogue often lies in the unexpected paths it may take and the novel viewpoints it uncovers.

Fostering Resilience through Respectful Discourse

Embracing the uncertain nature of discourse often demands resilience. In the steadfast commitment to understanding and growth, **it is crucial to foster an environment where respectful disagreement is not only tolerated but encouraged**. This ensures that the exchange, even when fraught with contention, remains grounded in mutual respect — a value deeply rooted in both spiritual and professional settings. **Aristotle once said, "*It is the mark of an educated mind to be able to entertain a thought without accepting it,*"** and this encapsulates the essence of resilience in debates — holding space for multiple potential truths and recognizing that the virtue lies in the exploration and examination.

The Legacy of Learned Conversations

In every conversation, you are contributing to your reputation and legacy — how you are perceived and the impact you make

on others. By adopting a growth mindset, you ensure this legacy is characterized by a commitment to learning and humility. *The stories we share about our experiences* not only humanize us but serve as practical examples of how dialogue can be both a learning opportunity and a tool for connection. **Let your dialogues be the kind that others recall as enriching and respectful**, where even the absence of agreement leaves a lasting impression of intellectual generosity and gracious discourse that leaves people open to converse with you again.

Practicing What We Preach

To engage authentically with the principles laid out here, practical application is essential. **Start small, if necessary. Engage with colleagues or friends with the explicit intent to listen and learn. Offer feedback that acknowledges different perspectives, and ask questions that propel the dialogue forward in constructive ways. Embrace the notion that being corrected is another opportunity for growth, and celebrate the courage it takes to revise one's stance in light of new evidence or better reasoning.** In doing so, you start to embody the very epitome of good sportsmanship in discourse — a stalwart advocate for growth, understanding and respect for one another.

Beyond Personal Affronts

In moving past the inclination to view disagreement as a personal slight, we mirror the call of Colossians 3:13, *"Bear with each other and forgive one another if any of you has a grievance against someone."* The cultivation of such an attitude requires us **not only**

to forgive but, fundamentally, to refrain from taking offense where no personal slight was intended.

To engage in discourse with grace and goodwill is to reflect the highest ideals of our shared spirituality, where each word exchanged is set against the benchmark of respect and an understanding of our shared humanity. We are co-travelers in the pursuit of truth, and it is in the courtesies we extend, the space we provide for varying voices and perspectives, that we honor this shared quest.

Growth Through Discourse, not Isolation

Every discussion becomes a classroom when approached with a growth mindset. Entrepreneurs and business leaders alike know this well; the marketplace of ideas, like any other market, thrives on innovation and adaptability. The most enduring success stories are those of individuals who saw beyond the lure of immediate validation, embracing instead the long-term value of enrichment through learning.

Remember the parable of the talents in Matthew 25:14-30; the master rewards those who use their resources to grow and multiply, rather than those who choose safety and stagnation. Similarly, we must invest our intellectual and spiritual assets in discussions that challenge and expand our horizons.

Our collective wisdom grows as we open our minds to the fresh winds of diverse opinions. **The resilience we build through such engagement is not just a personal gain but a contribution to the greater good, fortifying society against the brittleness of echo chambers and dogmatic rigidity.**

The Path Forward

Let us, therefore, set forth with a renewed commitment to embrace the dynamic interplay of ideas. **Let us approach our conversations with humility, understanding that our differences are not impediments but instruments of enlightenment, connection and reconciliation**. And let us extend the hand of fellowship, knowing that in the grand design, each voice adds depth to the chorus of human endeavor.

As we forge ahead in our dialogues, let our hearts rejoice in the knowledge that with every word exchanged in earnest, we move closer to bridging the chasms that divide us. It is in this noble pursuit that we find not only personal growth but also the means to knit together the fabric of a society rich in thought, robust in discourse, and resolute in togetherness.

9

AFTER THE DEBATE: AFFIRMATION AND INCLUSION

In the sunlit atrium of a bustling start-up incubator, where the air buzzed with the muted clatter of a dozen keyboards, Marcus sat at his desk, fingers still but mind racing. The morning's meeting had left a tense cloud hovering in the once relaxed office space — the kind of tension that comes not from enmity but from passionate discord, where visions align but roads diverge. His disagreement with Elena, his business partner, had been about the path their company should take, yet Marcus pondered on deeper rifts that such disagreements could cause in their relationship.

The light filtered through the tall glass panes, casting geometric shadows across his workspace. He recalled a passage that had steadied his heart in times of strife, *"As iron sharpens iron, so one person sharpens another,"* echoing from the spiritual teachings that bound his worldview. Marcus knew too well that conflict, when approached with respect and humility, forges stronger bonds, both in business and the personal sphere.

Marcus rose from his chair and walked towards the common area where sunlight pooled on leather couches and the air smelled like freshly brewed coffee mixed with a subtle hint of ambition. The clink of mugs and the soft laughter of his colleagues offered him a somber smile. To affirm someone's value post-debate, he thought, was less a task and more an art — a conscious offering of respect silhouetted against the backdrop of disagreement.

Elena stood near the window, her gaze lingering on the streets below, where the world moved unabated by the microcosm of their disagreement. He approached her, mind weaving a motivational tapestry to mend the cracks formed that morning.

Conflict was no stranger to Marcus's life; he lived by the belief that it was through the grind of opposing forces that wisdom was polished and purpose honed. His presence commanded attention, not due to volume but to the quiet certainty with which he spoke, "Elena, the worth of our partnership is not measured by consensus but by the bridges we build from different shores."

He had learned that the most profound growth often sprouted from the seeds of dissent, tended with patience and unwavering belief in a shared vision. Their company was more than a profit-and-loss statement; it was a testament to the confluence of diverse thought, a belief system in miniature borne of their united entrepreneurship.

Elena turned, her eyes not cold but contemplative, reflecting the same respect that Marcus endeavored to convey.

As the hubbub of the world outside continued its endless rhythm, within the incubator, two minds reached across the divide — a testament to the power of reaffirmation after confrontation. Would their relationship, tempered by discord, morph into an unbreakable alloy, exemplifying the strength of unified diversity?

The Power of Post-Conflict Affirmation

Understanding the significance of preserving relationships in the wake of disagreements is vital in both personal and professional realms. By expressing deep respect and love for individuals after an intellectual clash, we lay the foundation for enduring bonds. This chapter delves into the nuances of securing the worth of personal connections amidst divergence, with an unwavering assurance in each individual's intrinsic value. These principles are timeless, echoing through spiritual teachings that emphasize unity and the golden rule of treating others with the dignity and consideration we expect for ourselves.

Real-world experiences teach us that the wake of an argument can often be more pivotal than the debate itself. It's the moment when relationships are either fortified or weakened. The strategies outlined in this section are designed to transform conflict into connection, establishing that the personal worth of an individual transcends the often transitory nature of dissent. Businesses thrive when team members feel valued and respected; thus, learning to weave affirmation into the fabric of post-debate interactions is not only spiritually sound but also practically advantageous.

Scriptural passages across faiths encourage believers to "speak truth in love," merging conviction with compassion. This harmonious approach to disagreement requires **a commitment to see beyond the immediate contention and recognize the enduring humanity in each participant**. In the business world, this translates to a culture where diverse thoughts can thrive and every voice is acknowledged, fostering innovation and trust. The tactics discussed here are rooted in spiritual wisdom and practical application, forming a blueprint for inclusion that can be implemented in boardrooms, debate rooms and living rooms alike.

Expressing affirmation isn't just an abstract concept; it's an actionable practice. Entrepreneurs and leaders can shape environments that celebrate diversity of thought by routinely acknowledging the contributions of their colleagues and loved ones, even when they challenge prevailing perspectives.

The determination to maintain respect for all individuals is as much a personal endeavor as it is a societal imperative. It calls for conscious action to reaffirm each individual's worth after a disagreement. By building these habits, individuals and organizations weave a societal tapestry that values thoughtful discourse, leading to a more inclusive and compassionate constituency.

In the realm of human relationships, the aftermath of a disagreement is often a true test of character and commitment to mutual respect. It's not merely the ability to engage in debate, but **the practice of expressing love and appreciation for individuals post-dispute that keeps the foundations of a relationship strong.** Forgiving, forgetting, and moving forward with greater mutual understanding should become our aim — both for personal peace and for the health of our relationships with our families, co-workers, friends, acquaintances and opponents.

One might find inspiration in the wisdom of spiritual texts, which often emphasize the importance of love and forgiveness. Echoing this sentiment, **affirming love and appreciation for someone after a disagreement doesn't signify a surrender of one's beliefs, but rather a declaration of the primacy of relationship over the individual argument.** Just as many faiths teach us to love our neighbors as ourselves, this principle should guide our interactions, especially after a clash of opinions.

In business, too, such a principle holds sway. **A leader who can navigate conflict and emerge with team relationships intact is more effective than one who wins arguments but loses the respect or morale of their team.** Affirming personal worth is not only a matter of goodwill; it is a savvy tactic that bolsters team coherence and productivity. A leader's expression of appreciation acts as a reaffirmation of each team member's vital role within the organization, regardless of differences in opinion.

Nurturing a Respectful Environment After Disagreements

Personal anecdotes underscore these principles in action. Reflect, perhaps, on a time when you were at odds with a colleague or friend. The path to mending the rift likely involved acknowledging the other person's feelings and viewpoints, ensuring they were heard. It was a gesture of respect, a fundamental signal that while perspectives differ, the shared bond remains valued. It's this same expression of care that helps heal and strengthen relationships in the long run.

The Delicate Art of Balancing Relationships and Debates

Drawing upon uncertainties from various fields such as theology and politics, where conflict is often part and parcel of the daily grind, one sees the regular practice of reaffirmation. **Politicians, for all their differences, are known to commend each other's dedication and service, acknowledging worth outside their debates.** While it may seem contradictory, this type of behavior models the **importance of**

separating the individual from the dispute, facilitating a culture of mutual respect.

Embracing such an approach in one's personal and professional life requires effort and mindfulness. It's about actively deciding to **focus on people rather than problems**, embracing the richness brought by differing perspectives rather than merely tolerating them. By reaffirming personal worth consistently, one fosters a culture of respect and inclusivity — a crucial element in any thriving community or organization.

Navigating past disagreement to the reaffirmation of appreciation doesn't mean shying away from debates or suppressing healthy dissent. On the contrary, **it's about elevating the discourse to a place where personal relationships aren't casualties of conflict, but rather are strengthened by it.** Constructive disagreement, followed by genuine affirmation, becomes an opportunity for growth—a hallmark of powerful and successful relationships.

As we reflect on these insights, let us turn our attention to the practical tactics that can help us implement this culture of reaffirmation and respect, where every individual feels valued irrespective of their stance on any particular issue.

The Delicate Art of Reaffirmation

In the aftermath of a heated debate, it is crucial to reaffirm the personal worth of those involved. This isn't merely a kind gesture; it is an essential tactic for maintaining the integrity and strength of any relationship. Whether in a personal setting at home with family or within the professional domain of the corporate workplace, the need to validate an individual's value remains the same. Theologians and scholars alike have long touted the wisdom of **separating the person**

from the argument. Spiritual texts often guide us to **love the sinner while hating the sin,** and this principle can be effectively adapted to our topic: **respect the debating partner, even if you reject their viewpoints**.

To implement this, **begin by offering genuine compliments that are unrelated to the debate. Praise their passion, acknowledge their intellect, or commend their commitment to their beliefs.** This shows that you respect them beyond the confines of disagreement and that their worth to you transcends differing opinions. In a business context, such an approach paves the way for future collaborations and ensures that dialogue remains open and productive.

Actions Speak Louder

Following a debate, a tangible gesture can speak volumes about your commitment to the relationship. **Consider extending an olive branch in the form of a coffee invitation, a collaborative opportunity, or simply a supportive message.** These actions signify your intent to move forward positively, irrespective of the conflict. They demonstrate that your appreciation for the person and your professional rapport are not contingent upon agreement but are founded on mutual respect and inclusiveness.

Within the realm of a faith-driven perspective, such actions reflect the spiritual tenet of unconditional love. This creates an environment where individuals feel secure and valued, fostering a culture where diverse thoughts are not just tolerated, but embraced.

Engage in Reflective Listening

An effective tactic in reaffirming the worth of your debate partner is engaging in reflective listening. After the debate, take time to reiterate their points back to them, showing that you have heard and understood their perspective. This practice exemplifies the teaching popularized by the late great author Dr. Stephen R. Covey of "seeking first to understand, then to be understood," fostering a sense of being heard and valued. By reflecting their arguments in a respectful manner, you convey that their thoughts merit consideration, even if you do not agree with them.

In business, alike in all human interactions, this strategy enhances trust. It is a clear indication that every perspective is important, potentially transforming a simple conversation into a learning experience for both parties.

Implement Empathy

Empathy is an indispensable tool in validating another person's feelings and experiences. Expressing empathy is often reflected in sacred scriptures as a virtue of the compassionate and the wise. After a disagreement, show that you can understand and relate to the emotions and motivations behind their viewpoint. Sincere empathy can bridge the gap created by contention, reminding both participants of the fundamental human experience that unites them.

In entrepreneurship, this personal touch is often the cornerstone of building long-standing business relationships. It underscores the fact that professional respect can be maintained despite inevitable differences in opinion or strategy.

Maintain Open Communication Channels

Never underestimate the power of consistent and open communication post-debate. **Reach out to clarify your intentions if you worry they may have been misunderstood. Silent gaps after an argument can lead to festering resentments or assumptions that may further damage the relationship.** By keeping the lines of communication open, you reassure the other person that their input remains welcome and valued.

In the professional world, this approach can mean the difference between a partnership that evolves and one that dissolves. Transparency and clarity are as much virtues in the business world as they are in spiritual communities, binding people together with the thread of trust and respect.

Sometimes You Win, Lose, or Tie

Post-debate, encourage both yourself and your counterpart to reflect on what you've learned from the experience. Discussions and arguments often offer valuable insights and opportunities for personal growth. By focusing on these positives, you reaffirm the value that each person brings to the table. **It's not always about who won or lost, but what was discovered in the process.**

"Sometimes when you win, you really lose. And sometimes when you lose, you really win. And sometimes when you win or lose, you actually tie, and sometimes when you tie, you actually win or lose. Winning or losing is all one organic mechanism, from which one extracts what one needs." — Gloria Clemente from the movie *White Men Can't Jump*

Continue to Show Respect

Even after the conversation has ended, **continue to show respect for your debate partner in how you speak of the debate to others. This holds especially true in professional settings where gossip or slander can easily undermine someone's reputation**. Upholding respect in public forums not only reflects on your integrity but also safeguards the dignity of others.

Ultimately, it's about creating an environment where differing voices are not just heard but appreciated, where debates do not end in division but in a deeper understanding of one another. By practicing these tactics of reaffirmation, we are not just preserving relationships; we are enriching them, allowing us to navigate a world of diverse opinions with grace and wisdom.

The Harmony Process Model

The ability to engage with one another, even in the face of sharp disagreements, is rooted in our collective desire for understanding and connection. The Harmony Process Model delineates a five-stage journey designed to help transform contentious debates into opportunities for growth and collaboration. Here we'll delve into each stage, focusing on how they interact to form a coherent strategy for fostering inclusiveness and respect.

Establishing a Safe Space

The foundational component of the Harmony Process Model is the creation of a safe space. **This goes beyond mere physical comfort**

and enters the realm of psychological security, where individuals are assured that their voices will be respected and their personhood valued. Ground rules and established norms form the bedrock of this space, guiding participants towards mutual respect. **Such rules might include agreeing to refrain from personal attacks, to listen without interruption, and to acknowledge the inherent dignity in each other's viewpoints.** In such an environment, defensiveness subsides, allowing openness and vulnerability to facilitate genuine and authentic dialogue.

Active Listening and Empathy

Once a safe space has been secured, the focus shifts to active listening and empathy. This stage is not about passive reception but active engagement with the speaker's ideas and emotions. **The listener's role is to deeply understand, even if they do not align with the other's perspective. It's about being present and approachable, recognizing that beneath the surface of disagreement often lie shared fears, hopes, and values**. By validating emotions and experiences regardless of differing opinions, connections are fostered that transcend the debate at hand.

Clarifying and Paraphrasing

After listening actively, comes the critical task of clarifying and paraphrasing. **We often assume we understand the other's point of view, but without expressing it in our own words and seeking confirmation, misinterpretations can easily persist.** The discipline of paraphrasing what has been heard not only helps in shared understanding but also **demonstrates to the other person that**

his or her message is important enough to be fully grasped. It is a tangible manifestation of respect and is essential to moving the conversation forward constructively.

Identifying Common Goals and Values

With a clear understanding in place, participants can begin identifying common goals and values. This step is the bridge from empathy to action, highlighting that **despite different opinions, there are often similar aspirations and principles at the core between the two of us. It's a unifying process that illuminates mutual interests and paves the way for collaborative problem solving.** These commonalities serve as a reminder that **the relationship is greater than the conflict**, reinforcing a sense of shared purpose.

Generating Creative Solutions

The culmination of the process is the stage of generating creative solutions. **This is where dialogue turns into a shared venture towards resolving the issues that sparked the debate.** Bringing diverse perspectives to the table often leads to creative, innovative outcomes that might not have surfaced in a more homogeneous group. The focus is on brainstorming ideas and embracing a wide range of possibilities, with the aim of developing practical, mutually agreeable strategies. **It's about finding a path forward that respects the contributions of all involved, creating a sense of accomplishment and partnership.**

The essence of the Harmony Process Model is not just in each individual component, but in how they flow into one another. Respectful establishment of dialogue sets the tone for empathetic listening, which in turn enhances understanding that fuels the discovery of commonalities. This shared foundation then opens the door to inventive solutions borne from the crucible of diverse thought. It's a dynamic interplay, adaptable to the rhythms and needs of each unique conflict.

The significance of this Process Model lies in its implementation. **As communities, workplaces, and families adopt these stages, a more inclusive and respectful culture takes root — one where the fear of dissent is replaced by the hope of synergy. Where arguments were previously the end of discussion, they now become the catalysts for deeper connections and novel pathways forward.** This model celebrates not just the resolution of arguments, but the growth and learning they can stimulate. By embracing this framework, you are not merely ensuring a more harmonious debate, you are actively participating in the construction of a society that thrives on diversity, reconciliation and partnership.

Affirmation as a Foundation for Stronger Bonds

In the fabric of our lives, disagreements are inevitable, as are the varied colors that make up a tapestry. But it is in the careful stitching of affirmation and respect post-disagreement that relationships are fortified. The sincere expression of love and appreciation for an individual, irrespective of differing views, is a spiritual directive echoed across religious texts. It echoes the Biblical wisdom of 1 Peter 4:8, which teaches that "*Above all, love each other deeply, because love covers over a multitude of sins.*"

Let us not merely speak of such love but act upon it. **This active affirmation serves as a balm, soothing the potential wounds that debates can inflict.** It underscores the inherent worth and dignity of every individual, an idea deeply rooted in the Judeo-Christian under-standing that each person is created in the image of God.

Reframing Disagreements as Opportunities

Harnessing conflict as a catalyst for growth is an act of resilience. It is about transforming the sparks of discord into illuminating lights of mutual understanding. As entrepreneurs and leaders, we are tasked with navigating through diverse opinions. We must see beyond the immediate fray of contention **to recognize the latent potential** for innovation and progress that differing perspectives offer. **Let us be steadfast in creating environments where debates are not feared for their potential to divide but embraced for their power to enrich and unify.**

Inclusivity: The Cornerstone of Progress

The cultivation of a culture of respect and inclusiveness is not a passive exercise. It requires active participation, **the building of bridges over the chasms that threaten to separate us**. This comes not only from a place of empathy but also from an understanding of the pragmatic necessity for synergy in a world where challenges are complex and multifaceted. As we integrate insights from theology, politics, and economics, we understand that true wisdom comes from the synthesis of diverse thoughts and experiences.

Our families, businesses, communities, and institutions thrive when they reflect the broad spectrum of human experi-ence. By fostering an environment of inclusivity, we unlock doors to uncharted avenues of thought, innovation, and connection. When we stand on the foundational truth that **every voice has value**, we rise together to the higher calling of mutual prosperity, stronger community and shared success.

The Path Forward

Let this chapter in our lives, then, not be one of division but a rallying cry for greater connection. **With each conversation, may we have the foresight to see the person before the position, the relationship before the resolution.** As we look ahead, **keep this affirmation at the forefront of your mind:** *"I value you. I respect our differences, and I am committed to moving forward together."*

Reflect on the tales of those who came before us; our ancestors, grandparents and parents navigated much rougher seas of disagreement and yet managed to chart a course towards unity and collaboration. Their stories, their lessons, are the beacons that guide us today. **Stand firm in the belief that every effort made to affirm, include, and respect, no matter how small, contributes to the greater composition of a harmonious society.**

As we embrace diversity of thought, let us not lose sight of the shared humanity that binds us all. Be bold, be courageous, and let the spirit of affirmation imbue every facet of your life — with peace, purpose, and a profound sense of connection.

10

THE REAL-WORLD PRACTICE OF CIVIL DISCOURSE

The morning light filtered through the stained windows of the café, casting a kaleidoscope of colors over the patrons gathered inside. Among them sat Benjamin, a man well past his youth, fingers interlocked and eyes heavy with reflections. He had an air of resolve, a silent commitment to a personal journey that few knew but many sensed. The worn leather of the booth creaked beneath him as he shifted, gathering his thoughts with the purpose of a man building a bridge between disparate shores.

Benjamin was a fixture in the community, known for his business acumen and his intricate understanding of how commerce, politics, and faith intertwine like the strands of a rope. In his mind, he was always balancing ledgers, not just of finances but of conversations, gauging the weight of words against the scales of civility. His latest venture, a program to foster dialogue among budding entrepreneurs from diverse backgrounds, gnawed at his conscience. The goal was ambitious: to promote a society where difference in thought did not mean discord but a symphony of ideas strengthening the whole.

A server, with a smile warm as the coffee she poured, interrupted his reverie. "Is there anything you need, Mr. Benjamin?" she asked.

"Thank you, my dear, I require nothing but the space to think," he responded, the corners of his eyes crinkling with a gratitude deeper than the simple exchange warranted. She, unknowing, was part of his mission, her questions and stories from the day were threads in the tapestry he hoped to weave.

Benjamin had witnessed the hardening of dialogue within business walls and the broader community. His own past — punctuated by moments of impassioned yet incendiary debates — served not as a beacon of righteousness but as humble pie on his road to mastering the art of civil discourse. How often had he brushed aside a differing opinion not with grace, but with the blunt force of his own perspective? Now he recognized such moments as then-unseen opportunities to harmonize rather than homogenize the rich tapestry of human experience.

As the morning bustle swirled around him, he penned his thoughts in a notebook weathered like an ancient scripture. Each word committed to the page was a manifesto of his personal transformation — a testament to the amalgamation of theology, economics, and the political whirlwinds that shape our every day. He noted, "In commerce and community alike, richness lies in variety; this café indulges the palate in the same way that society should indulge a plurality of thought."

Fully immersed once again in his inner dialogue, Benjamin pondered on the practical steps that he might take to enshrine these values into the core of his new program. He thought of integrating mentorship sessions, where seasoned entrepreneurs would embody the spirit of civil discourse, mentoring not by preaching, but by engaging in genuine and respectful exchange.

Just as a mentor would weave tales to illuminate a point, so did Benjamin plan to illustrate his lessons through personal anecdotes. He understood the power of a well-placed story to impart deep understanding. "Stories," he mused, "are the currency of human connection, as valuable in teaching as any textbook or ledger."

Sipping his coffee, its bitterness reminding him of past missteps and its warmth promising the potential of the future, Benjamin gazed at the bustling street outside. People hurried by, each engrossed in their own narrative and agenda, yet part of a larger communal story.

What would it take, he wondered, for society to fully embrace the continuous journey towards mastering civil discourse? How might we all begin to see the value in every voice, to turn discord into a tapestry, filled with the vibrant threads of disparate life experiences, cultures, thoughts, beliefs and votes?

The Ongoing Odyssey of Civil Discourse

Mastering the art of civil discourse is not an achievement you neatly pack away on a shelf, like a diploma that testifies to a job well done. It is a quest without end — dynamic, indispensable, and enriching to those who journey through its practice. Acknowledgment of this voyage as a lifelong commitment is the bedrock upon which civil societies are built. It requires us to weave empathy, respect, and understanding into the very fabric of our interactions. **In a world brimming with diverse opinions, the challenge before us is not merely to coexist, but to converge in a harmonious symphony of dissenting voices**. Such convergence is not only possible but essential; it requires us to elevate our dialogues from clashing noises to a dialogue of depth and resonance.

The preceding chapters of this book have laid a foundation for understanding why the embrace of diverse thought is indispensable in a polarized world. Here, in this crucial segment of our exploration, we focus on the linchpin of our shared human experience: the practice of civil discourse. **Our charge is to mold this practice into an integral part of our everyday lives, etching commitment to a journey of ongoing improvement into our character and within our interpersonal relationships.** By undertaking this journey boldly and relentlessly, we envision a society where divergent perspectives no longer fragment but, instead, fortify the common good.

The Sacred Path of Understanding

Ingrained within the teachings of sacred texts and spiritual leaders is a call to seek understanding, nurture inclusivity, and promote unity without uniformity. It's a testament that civil discourse moves beyond a mere skill — it's a personal and spiritual **commitment to walk alongside others, even when the path diverges**. As we outline steps to fortify this practice, remember that these are illuminated by age-old wisdom that has guided civilizations towards peace and cooperation since time immemorial.

Harness Empathy Amidst Discord

Creating a safe environment is your first step towards empathetic encounters — a simple act that can bridge worlds. It's about fostering a space where differing voices are not just heard but felt, laying a foundation for connection. A safe space is a sanctuary from the tempest of divisiveness and closed-mindedness, offering solace in understanding a world too often cold and insensitive to the nuances of human experience.

In **attentively listening**, we affirm the dignity of the speaker and the value of his or her perspective. It's an active, arduous undertaking that requires the full arsenal of our attention. But the rewards transcend the mere exchange of words; they cement the bonds of respect essential for any thriving democracy.

Validating emotions is no less critical. It's acknowledging that beneath the husk of our arguments lay the beating hearts of human emotions. By recognizing these, we engage not just with ideas but with the people behind them, reinforcing the notion that we share a fundamental, human connection that outstrips disagreement.

Armed with empathy, **reflect and paraphrase** the shared thoughts — a mirror to the soul that says, "I see you, I hear you." This reciprocal gaze, the act of reflecting back what has been shared, is a cornerstone of understanding and trust-building. It is a validation that the speaker's narrative bears worth and significance.

Asking open-ended questions is not a means to an end but an invitation to a journey. Cutting through the superficial, these questions probe deeper, drawing out a fuller portrait of the personal landscapes from which our varied perspectives arise.

Sharing your perspective with empathy requires meticulous articulation — it is to navigate the delicate vicissitudes of human feelings with the precision of a surgeon. By framing our narratives with care and consideration, focusing just as much on how we share our perspectives as the actual words coming out of our mouths, we eschew the armor of hostility and extend an olive branch that says, "Your story matters, and here is mine."

Forging Agreement in Adversity

To **seek common ground** is to see through the prism of our shared humanity. It is a conscientious choice to look beyond the immediate and to see the potential for unification even in the midst of our most daunting differences. Touching upon shared values and aspirations, we create a cornerstone for collaboration and co-creation.

The practice doesn't end when the conversation does. **Self-reflection** is the silent interlocutor, the voice within that constantly challenges us to grow, evolve, and transcend our previous limitations. Self-reflection is not merely a luxury — it's a necessity for those who dare to better themselves, their families, their communities and society.

The Compass of Conversation

As we near the culmination of our literary journey together, let's reflect on how the principles within these pages seek to infuse your life with empathy, equip you with the functional artisanry of dialogue, and ultimately, guide you to masterful civil discourse. Time has been spent dissecting the 5-step *Disagree without Disrespect* framework, an architectural marvel designed to craft conversations that are as constructive as they are transformative. This framework not just safeguards relationships but enriches them, fostering an environment where tolerance, respect, and genuine curiosity become the foundation of every interaction.

Now, as you close the covers of this book and step back out into the real world, it is your actions that will etch the lasting impact of these words into the annals of time. The journey towards harmonizing dissent begins with a step, a word, a breath — each a symphony waiting to be composed through the practice of civil discourse. As you embark on this odyssey, embed the principles into the very essence of your life's work, and watch as the ripples from your commitment to understanding transform the seas of discord into oceans of possibility.

Embracing the dynamic nature of civil discourse mirrors the commitment one must bring to any significant area of personal development. Much like committing to physical fitness or professional growth, becoming adept at engaging in respectful, meaningful conversations across divides is not a one-time event but an ever-unfolding path. **Civil discourse is not simply about being amiable or avoiding disagreements; indeed, it is a sophisticated skill set that involves active listening, empathetic engagement, and the thoughtful articulation of one's own perspective.**

What defines mastery in this realm is not the absence of conflict, but the capacity to navigate it with grace and constructive intent. It is about fostering an environment where discussions are not defined by the pressure to win, but by a collective pursuit of understanding and progress. The increasing polarization in today's society demands that individuals not only understand the principles of productive dialogue but commit to refining their abilities consistently and conscientiously.

References to esteemed spiritual teachings may offer guidance for how one should engage with diverse viewpoints. We may find solace and instruction in the wisdom of texts that call for love, patience, and understanding as pathways to greater harmony. In the practice of civil discourse, it becomes essential to approach each conversation with the intent of learning rather than persuading, extending the kindness and respect often elucidated in our most revered spiritual philosophies.

For those in the business world, the value of civil discourse lies not only in its ethical merit but also in its practical advantages. **Negotiations and leadership require a keen ability to engage others constructively, persuade ethically, and foster collaborative solutions. Adopting civil discourse as a core component of one's professional demeanor can significantly enhance both individ-**

ual and organizational effectiveness. A personal anecdote may underline this point: a business leader who transitions from commanding to conversing with their team may see a remarkable increase in productivity, innovation, and overall workplace morale.

However, recognizing the importance of civil discourse is not enough if we do not put it into practice. It is one matter to nod in agreement with its principles, and quite another to demonstrate patience and openness when faced with opposing views. Encounters that challenge our beliefs and convictions can serve as practical exercises in applying our commitment to civil discourse. **The ultimate test, and opportunity for growth, is found in the heat of disagreement and the temptation to revert to adversarial defaults.**

To enrich the practice, engage with a variety of perspectives. Delve into different fields such as theology, politics, and economics to understand how civil discourse shapes these arenas. Analyze case studies where open dialogue has led to breakthroughs, and draw inspiration from the annals of history where spirited debate underpinned some of the greatest advancements of human civilization. **By appreciating how our conduct in conversation can influence outcomes in various contexts, we deepen our dedication to refining our discourse.**

Approach this ongoing journey with the patience and persistence of a mentor, understanding that every interaction is an occasion to learn and improve. Share your progress and setbacks with a friend or an accountability partner, and let these experiences be both a lesson and encouragement to others. In doing so, you become an active participant in not just enhancing your own skills, but also modeling them for those within your influence.

Now, as we strive to increase our proficiency in civil discourse, let us acknowledge that it is not simply an individual endeavor, but a communal one. Our efforts ripple outward, touching the lives of everyone we interact with and contributing to the broader social fabric.

Developing a Lifelong Commitment to Civil Discourse

Commitment is the bedrock on which the edifice of civil discourse is built. **Embracing the continuous journey of mastering civil discourse is akin to the dedication required in nurturing a relationship or honing a valued skill. A personal vow to engage thoughtfully, listen respectfully, and communicate empathetically is not an achievement marked by finality but rather an ongoing aspiration.** By internalizing revered spiritual teachings which extol the virtues of patience, kindness, compassion, unconditional love towards one another and mutual understanding, we lay the groundwork for a discourse that is enriched with a depth of perspective and a heart for learning.

In the realm of business and entrepreneurship, a pledge to improve discourse represents an investment in one's professional and personal growth. Effective communication serves as a cornerstone for successful leadership and negotiation, fostering a climate where ideas can be exchanged and progress can be made. Just as an entrepreneur invests time and resources into a startup, investing in the refinement of one's dialogue capabilities can yield significant dividends. This calls for an unwavering commitment to practice and self-improvement, recognizing that the fruits of such labor may take time to manifest.

Drawing from my own experiences in leadership roles, I have come to appreciate the subtle yet profound impact that a commitment to civil discourse can have on team dynamics. Meetings transformed into collaborative sessions rather than adversarial debates when all voices were acknowledged and considered. This shift did not occur overnight; it was the product of consistent, deliberate practice and an openness to learning from every interaction. This anecdote underscores the practical reality: applying a dedicated growth mindset to the art of civil discourse can tangibly improve our interactions and relationships.

Balancing the demands of professionalism while fostering a spirit of approachable communication is essential. Expressing oneself with clarity and conciseness does not preclude warmth but rather ensures that messages are understood and appreciated. Through interactions that display genuine interest and respect for differing viewpoints, a professional is seen not just as a master of his or her craft but as a visionary who cherishes the mosaic of human experience.

Integration of diverse insights from theology to politics and economics is crucial in understanding the intricate tapestry of human discourse. Acknowledging and applying principles from these varied fields encourages a well-rounded, informed approach to conversation that is both enlightening and beneficial. By looking at case studies where a commitment to communication has bridged seemingly insurmountable divides, we gain inspiration and practical strategies for our own encounters.

Establishing a personal rapport with your audience requires sharing resonant stories that reflect shared struggles and triumphs. In my journey, there have been moments of intense frustration and profound breakthroughs, all centered around the challenging yet rewarding task of engaging in thoughtful dialogue. Through these shared experiences, we recognize the value of our individual commitment to this practice — it's not just a solitary venture but a collective stride towards better understanding.

Engagement in civil discourse is not a matter of mere politeness but a strategic choice for those who wish to lead and influence effectively in the home, in the workplace, in the boardroom, in the place of worship, in the community center, and in the political arena. It requires a resolve that must be renewed with each conversation, a passion for the common good that outshines the temptation to win an argument while looking superior over your opponent, and an understanding that the harmony created through mutual respect is far more valuable than the hollow victory of a one-sided battle.

By embracing this journey wholeheartedly, with eyes wide open to the challenges and hearts full of the potential rewards, we position ourselves not only as learners but as bridge builders — architects of a future where discourse is the bridge that connects rather than a barrier that divides. Let these words not merely be read but be acted upon, for it is action that breeds change, and it is change that fosters harmony.

A Symphony of Voices

In the grand orchestra of society, each individual's voice acts as a distinct instrument, contributing unique tones to the collective harmony. Just as in music, civil discourse allows for the blending of these diverse sounds into a melody richer and more complex than any single note could achieve. **Our responsibility, then, is to learn how to play our parts with both passion and restraint, always mindful of the overarching composition**. When we appreciate the symphony of voices around us, we contribute to a society that is more empathetic, understanding, and enriched by its differences. This practice, not unlike the rehearsal of an ensemble, requires us to hone our skills continually, to listen intently, and to contribute thoughtfully.

The Path of Personal Commitment

Walking the path of civil discourse demands a personal commitment to growth and adaptability. It calls for self-reflection and an unwavering dedication to understanding others. Here, our spiritual teachings offer guidance, reminding us to *"do unto others as you would have them do unto you"* (Luke 6:31). In the business context, this translates to fostering networks and collaborations that thrive on mutual respect and the knowledge that diversity of thought propels innovation and progress. As individuals, each step forward on this journey enhances our own discourse skills and positions us as role models within our communities and circles of influence.

Catalyzing Positive Change

Your voice has the power to catalyze change, and with each conversation, you pave the way for a more inclusive society. To **reframe debates as opportunities** rather than obstacles is to pave the way for transformation. By practicing patience and open-mindedness, we encourage others to express themselves without fear of derision or dismissiveness. This not only deepens connections but also establishes a culture where **collaboration triumphs over conflict**. As leaders, entrepreneurs, and influencers, the onus falls upon us to champion this vision and demonstrate the advantages that arise when diverse perspectives are not just tolerated but wholeheartedly embraced.

A Call for Collaborative Wisdom

In a world brimming with opinions and data, fostering a space where these can converge for the greater common good is essential. Theology, politics, economics — each provides a slice of the greater puzzle. Imagine the insights that could be gleaned if they were all viewed not as competing ideologies but as **collaborative pieces of wisdom**, each offering a path to better understanding the human condition. This is the ideal of harmonized diversity: different strands of thought interwoven to strengthen the fabric of discourse and decision-making that benefits us as a community.

Enduring Grace in Adversity

Undoubtedly, the journey is riddled with challenges. You may encounter skeptical resistance, and conversations may at times escalate despite your best efforts. Here, enduring grace becomes a beacon. **It is the grace to remain composed, the courage to stay the course, and the wisdom to know that every moment of adversity is an opportunity to practice the art of civil discourse**. By embodying these qualities, we encourage others to do the same, fostering an environment where discourse is defined by dignity and poise.

The Vital Role of Empathy

Empathy is the cornerstone of productive dialogue. **By striving to see the world through the eyes of others, we build bridges across ideological divides.** Real-world experiences, when shared with empathy, have the power to resonate deeply, convincing others of our sincerity and commitment to mutual understanding. **Such vulnerability in conversation can transform competitors into collaborators, opponents into partners.** Thus, integrating empathy into our communication is not just a technique — it's an essential strategy for advancing collective enlightenment.

Solidifying Connection Through Action

Taking action is foundational to solidifying the bonds formed through civil discourse. It is one thing to speak of unity and understanding, and quite another to demonstrate these principles through our deeds. **By actively participating in community dialogues, supporting initiatives that promote thoughtful debate, and mentoring the next generation in the lifelong skills of civil discourse, we manifest our dedication to the practice.** This tangible engagement not only enriches our personal experiences but also echoes outward, serving as a testament to the power of constructive, civic conversation.

A Commitment to Continual Learning

No expert musician ever rests on their laurels. They practice, they perform, they learn, and they grow. Similarly, the mastery of civil discourse is an evolving art that benefits from continual learning and exposure to new ideas and perspectives. **Reading widely from varied sources, attending forums and workshops, and seeking diverse interactions are all part of this educational process.** The more we learn from different sources and perspectives, the more adept we become at navigating the complexities of human dialogue, and the better we can serve as harmonious contributors to society's ever-unfolding narrative.

The Journey Continues

Mastering civil discourse is not a destination; it's a journey. Much like a seed that needs water, sunlight, and care to become a mighty oak, **the practice of civil discourse requires dedication, persistence, and adaptation over time**. As we navigate through conversations rife with diversity, let us remember that the principles of empathy and respect are not one-time achievements but perpetual commitments.

A Personal Covenant

Our society thrives when individuals take it upon themselves to grow and improve. **Imagine if every leader, entrepreneur, and citizen viewed their communication skills as an ever-evolving craft.** Making a personal commitment to cultivating these skills is a testament to one's integrity and respect for others. Reflect upon this truth: *"He who restrains his words has knowledge, and he who has a cool spirit is a man of understanding."* (Proverbs 17:27). Let this wisdom guide our daily interactions with one another.

Building Bridges, Not Walls

The art of thoughtful debate is an essential cornerstone in a society that values freedom and growth. It is not enough to simply coexist with different opinions; we must strive to integrate them into a beautiful mosaic representing humanity's collective wisdom. Imagine a business environment where constructive discourse leads to innovation instead of conflict. Such a society fosters a synergy that turns the cacophony of dissenting voices into a harmonious dialogue, benefiting all.

Empowerment Through Action

As we close this chapter, let it serve as a catalyst for your continued effort in refining discourse. **Challenge yourself to engage with perspectives that differ from your own, and do so with the spirit of understanding, not the intent to refute.** Just as the experienced craftsman sharpens his tools, **sharpen your mind** with every discussion, every debate, every peaceful exchange of ideas.

The Art of Meaningful Connection

Let each conversation you embark upon be tinged with the authenticity and caring of a heart-to-heart exchange. Share your stories and listen earnestly to others, for it is only through genuine connection that we can hope to transform conflict into connection.

The Masterful Dance of Discourse

Embrace the dynamism and subtleties of civil discourse as if you were learning the steps to an intricate dance. Light on your feet and clear in your mind, you can then navigate the complex terrain of human interaction with grace and ease.

By consistently applying the **5-step *Disagree without Disrespect* framework** discussed in this book, you will have equipped yourself with an invaluable toolkit to engage in civil discourse. You will **emerge** more measured, more persuasive, and more connected with the world around you. May this book serve as your **compass**, guiding you towards ever more meaningful and respectful conversations.

The Nexus of Connection: A Guiding Compass for Contentious Times

As we journey through the tempestuous seas of dialogue, engaged in the ebbs and flows of passionate dissent, may we emerge harbored in the sanctuary of mutual understanding and respect. This book's mission has been to chart a course to such a haven, guiding you to navigate the waters of disagreement with grace and irrefutable purpose. As we conclude this voyage, let us reflect on the quintessence of our shared exploration and how its principles can illuminate the path ahead in your daily interactions and ambitions.

The real-world applications of this book are numerous and profound. In workplaces bustling with a convergence of cultures and opinions, you can deftly transform conflict into a crucible for creativity and innovation. In town halls and communities divided, you can be the linchpin of unity, fostering dialogues that evolve into harmonious action. Within the sacred walls of friendship and family, where differences might once have threatened to erode bonds, you can now sow the seeds of deeper understanding and affection.

Let us briefly recapitulate: **Embrace the diversity of thought as a gift,** not a curse. **Listen** with the intent to understand, not merely to reply. Engage in **dialogue** with a spirit of **humility**, recognizing that in the vast expanse of knowledge, we all hold but a candle's light. Craft your arguments with **respectful** artistry, **weaving evidence and empathy** into a tapestry that **invites reflection, not rebuke**. And finally, **seek the common ground**, however elusive it might appear, for it is upon this shared earth that the garden of community thrives.

The journey to mastering the art of thoughtful debate is a lifelong pursuit. You have accessed a foundation from which to launch — a 5-step *Disagree without Disrespect* framework — but the edifice you construct upon it will be uniquely your own. **Continue to practice**, **reflect**, and **refine** your approach as you encounter each new discourse and personality. The recommendations laid forth are your instruments; use them to craft symphonies of consensus and concertos of mutual progress.

Every work has its limitations, and mine is no exception. Fruitful avenues for further exploration abound. How might we amplify the voices of the underrepresented in our dialogues? How can technology serve not as a barrier but as a bridge in our conversations? These questions and many more beckon us toward a horizon rich with possibility. Keep learning and applying what you learn.

Now, empowered with the insights this book has provided, **I urge you to take action**. Let the reverberations of your learned discourse echo in dining rooms, boardrooms, sanctuaries, and public squares. Change begins with the individual; **be the herald of civil dialogue and the ambassador of tempered debate in your sphere of influence.**

As you embark on this noble endeavor, remember that **you are divinely equipped for this mission**. You carry within you the immeasurable capacity for growth and the will to build a legacy that honors the Creator of all. In every exchange, may your words be seasoned with grace, an offering pleasing and sacrosanct.

In closing, let me leave you with a lasting impression: **your words have the power to wound or heal, to separate or unify**. Your tongue is a flame — wield it with sacred caution and intentional benevolence. Speak life over death in your discussions, debates and relationships.

As an influential under-shepherd of old once penned:

"Let your speech always be gracious, seasoned with salt, so that you may know how you ought to answer each person." — Colossians 4:6

Go forth with this wisdom as your guide, for even in dissent, there exists the potential for a perfect harmony that resounds to the heavens. May God bless you.

ABOUT THE AUTHOR

What is most important to Philip Blackett and what truly forms his identity is his relationship with his Lord and Savior Jesus Christ. Philip's mission for the rest of his life is to Grow God's People, Grow God's Businesses, and Grow God's Kingdom as a good and faithful steward of all God has entrusted him, while having a positive influence on all who he encounters each day as a Kingdom Man.

Professionally speaking, Philip is passionate about helping entrepreneurs and small business owners grow their dream businesses, while utilizing his skillset in sales, marketing and business development. Previously, Philip served as President of Cemetery Services, Inc., a seven-figure business he bought based in the Greater Boston area. It was "his pleasure" to also serve as a Manager for a Chick-Fil-A restaurant.

At FedEx, Philip previously provided support to several senior Marketing executives (including the current CEO) as a Senior Communications Specialist after working on its Corporate Social Responsibility team. Before FedEx, Philip advised investors on Wall Street in New York City as an Equity Research Analyst for Goldman Sachs, where he helped recommend investments in over 100 publicly traded companies across ten industries.

Regarding his education, Philip graduated from the Southern Baptist Theological Seminary with his Masters of Divinity (M.Div) degree with a concentration in Great Commission Studies. He also earned his MBA from Harvard Business School. In college, Philip graduated from the University of North Carolina at Chapel Hill as a Morehead-Cain Scholar, majoring in Political Science and Economics.

Philip is a Life Member of Alpha Phi Alpha Fraternity, Inc. When he is not actively fulfilling his mission, Philip enjoys reading, watching sports, and raising his twin daughters, Sofia and Elizabeth, with his wife Mayra.

BOOKS BY PHILIP

Disagree without Disrespect: How to Respectfully Debate with Those who Think, Believe and Vote Differently than You

Future-Proof: How to Adopt and Master Artificial Intelligence (A.I.) to Secure Your Job and Career

The Unfair Advantage: How Small Business Owners can Use Artificial Intelligence (A.I.) to Boost Sales, Outsmart the Competition and Grow their Dream Businesses without Breaking the Bank

Jesus over Black: How My Faith Transformed Me into a Conservative within the Black Community

Maverick Lineage: What I Learned about Black Conservatism in America

Bridging the GOP Gap: How the Republican Party can Win Over African American Voters with Inclusivity and Trust without Compromising Values

CONNECT WITH PHILIP

f

facebook.com/PhilipBlackettFB

🐦

twitter.com/PhilipBlackett

in

linkedin.com/in/philipblackett

📷

instagram.com/philipblackett

▶

youtube.com/@PhilipBlackett

♪

tiktok.com/@pblackett

Facebook:

https://www.facebook.com/PhilipBlackettFB

X (Twitter):

https://twitter.com/PhilipBlackett

LinkedIn:

https://www.linkedin.com/in/philipblackett

Instagram:

https://instagram.com/philipblackett

YouTube:

https://www.youtube.com/@PhilipBlackett

TikTok:

https://www.tiktok.com/@pblackett

Blog:

https://www.PhilipBlackett.com

Made in United States
Orlando, FL
29 July 2024

49672687R00093